P9-BZP-030

COCOA

AND

CHOCOLATE

THE CHOCOLATE GIRL — BY LIOTARD.

FROM THE ORIGINAL PAINTING IN THE DRESDEN GALLERY.

THE REGISTERED TRADE-MARK OF WALTER BAKER & CO., U.S.A.

COCOA

AND

CHOCOLATE

A SHORT HISTORY OF THEIR
PRODUCTION AND USE

WITH A FULL AND PARTICULAR ACCOUNT OF THEIR
PROPERTIES, AND OF THE VARIOUS METHODS
OF PREPARING THEM FOR FOOD

APPLEWOOD BOOKS
CARLISLE, MASSACHUSETTS

Cocoa and Chocolate
was originally published in 1886.

978-1-4290-9375-0

Thank you for purchasing an Applewood book. Applewood reprints
America's lively classics—books from the past that are still of interest to
modern readers. Our mission is to build a picture of America's past through
its primary sources. To inquire about this edition or to request a free copy of
our current catalog featuring our best-selling books, write to:

Applewood Books
P.O. Box 27
Carlisle, MA 01741

For more complete listings, visit us on the web at: www.awb.com

MANUFACTURED IN THE UNITED STATES OF AMERICA

CONTENTS.

—◦◦—

SOURCES OF INFORMATION.

"A New Survey of the West Indies," etc., by Thomas Gage. 2d edition, London, 1655.

"The Natural History of Chocolate," by a French Officer; translated by Dr. R. Brookes, and printed in London, 1730.

"Foods": (International scientific series), by Dr. Edward Smith, London, 1873.

"The Beverages we Infuse": Blackwood's Magazine, v. 75, 1854.

"Physiologie du Goût," by J. Anthelme Brillat-Savarin. New edition, 2 v., Paris.

"Le Cacao et le Chocolat, considerés aux points de vue botanique, chimique, physiologique, agricole, commercial, industrial et economique." Par Arthur Mangin, Paris, 1862.

"A Practical Treatise on the Analysis of Tea, Coffee, Cocoa, Chocolate, etc.," by J. Alfred Wanklÿn, Public Analyst, etc., London, 1874.

" McCulloch's Dictionary of Commerce and Commercial Navigation," London, 1882.

" Spon's Encyclopædia of the Industrial Arts," etc., Div. II., London, 1880.

" Encyclopædia Britannica," 9th edition, Article " Cocoa."

Lecture on " Chocolate," before the Sheffield Scientific School, New Haven, 1881, by Professor Daniel C. Eaton.

" A Manual of Hygiene," prepared especially for use in the medical service of the army, by Edmund A. Parkes, M.D., F.R.S., London, 1864.

" A Treatise on Hygiene and Public Health," edited by Albert H. Buck, M.D., New York, 1879.

The " Cantor" Lectures on Food, by H. Letheby, London, 1872.

" Cocoa," by John R. Jackson.   " Nature," v. 2, 1870.

" Adulterations of Food," by Rowland J. Atcherly, Ph.D., London, 1874.

" Lectures on Diet and Regimen," by A. F. M. Willick, M.D., 3d edition, London, 1801.

Paper on " Chocolate," in the " Annales de Physique et de Chimie," by M. Boussingault, member of the French Institute.

" History of American Manufactures," by J. L. Bishop.

Reports on Commerce and Navigation, and Consular Reports, United States and Great Britain.

Works on Cookery, by Maria Parloa, Pierre Caron, Pierre Blot, Mrs. M. F. Henderson, Marion Harland, Flora Neely, Matilda Lees Dods, Mrs. Blair, Sara T. Paul; also, the "Confectioner's Journal," "The Dessert Book," "Choice Receipts," etc.

COCOA AND CHOCOLATE.

I.

CONSUMPTION

DURING the last half-century the consumption of cocoa in various forms has increased to an extraordinary extent, both in this country and Great Britain. This is due to several causes, among the most prominent of which are, (1) a reduction in the retail price, which brings it within the means of the poorer classes; (2) a more general recognition of the value of cocoa as an article of diet, and (3) improvements in methods of preparation, by which it is adapted to the wants of different classes of consumers.

There is no doubt that, if it had not been for the monopoly of the production which Spain long possessed, and which kept the price, on its first introduction into England, at a point where only the rich could afford to buy it, cocoa would have come into as general use there as it did in Spain, and would, perhaps, have been received with more favor than tea or coffee, which were introduced about the same time.

It appears that, in the time of Charles II., the price of the best chocolate (very crude, undoubtedly, as compared with the present manufactures), was 6s. 8d. a pound, which, if we take into account the greater purchasing power of money at that time, would be equal to at least $5 a pound at this time for a coarse compound.

Humboldt estimated the consumption of cocoa in Europe, in 1806, at 23,000,000 pounds per annum, of which from 6,000,000 to 9,000,000 were supposed to be consumed in Spain. From the latest official returns of imports and consumption in the principal countries it appears that over 70,000,000 pounds are now used. France heads the list with 26,750,250 pounds ; Spain comes next, with 16,450,000 ; England consumes 13,966,512 ; the Netherlands, 5,475,000 ; Germany, about 3,250,000, and Belgium, 1,245,000. The United States stands next to Great Britain in the list of consumers, the amount of crude cocoa entered for consumption last year being about 8,500,000 pounds. The returns of exportations from the countries in which the article is produced are so incomplete that it is impossible to state definitely the total amount exported ; but it is probably not far from 80,000,000 pounds per annum. Reckoning the consumption in the countries where it is raised at not less than 20,000,000 pounds, it may safely be assumed that the total annual product does not fall short of 100,000,000 pounds.

While the average price of the raw product has steadily increased during the last
thirty years (from 47s. per cwt., between
1854–60, to 74s. between 1881–84[1]), the
retail price of the prepared cocoa has
fallen. This is due to improvements in
machinery and methods of handling, and
to the sharp competition between the leading manufacturers.

In 1820 the quantity of cocoa entered for
home consumption in the United Kingdom
of Great Britain and Ireland was only
267,321 pounds; in 1884 it amounted to
13,966,512 pounds of crude cocoa, and
1,033,173 pounds of chocolate, — in all
about 15,000,000 pounds, an increase of
5,500 per cent. in sixty-four years. The
population, in the meantime, had increased
only 73¾ per cent. ; the use of tea had increased only 457 per cent., and of coffee
only 356 per cent.   During the last twenty-

---

[1] Mulhall's (English) Price Lists.

five years the consumption of cocoa and its products in the United Kingdom has increased about 230 per cent. The consumption per inhabitant is about 6³/₅ oz.

In the United States the increased consumption in recent years has been no less striking. The amount of cocoa retained for home consumption in 1860 was only 1,181,054 pounds; in 1885 it was 8,426,787 pounds (that is, cocoa, crude cocoa and shells, not including chocolate, which is classed, in the official returns of imports, under the general head of "farinaceous articles"), — an increase of 614 per cent. in twenty-five years. The population increased during that period less than 60 per cent. The consumption of tea increased 153 per cent., and of coffee 196 per cent.

In view, therefore, of the great and constantly increasing use of this product, its properties and supply become questions of the highest economic and hygienic importance. For the purpose of satisfying

the desire for information upon a subject
which is of such general interest we have
collected, from the most authentic sources,
such facts in relation to the growth of
the cacao-tree, the preparation of its fruit for
the market, and the value of the different
preparations for dietary purposes, as may
serve to increase the common stock of
knowledge in regard to one of the staple
articles of food.

II.

THE CACAO—TREE.

THE term " Cocoa " is a corruption of " Cacao," but is almost universally used in English-speaking countries. The cacao-tree belongs to the natural order of Sterculiaceæ, — a family of about 41 genera and 521 species, inhabiting the warmer regions of the world. None of them grow naturally in our climate, or in Europe, and, excepting the little yellow-flowered Mahernie, they are very seldom seen in our conservatories.

The cacao-tree can be cultivated in suitable situations within the 25th parallels of latitude. It flourishes best, however, within the 15th parallels, at elevations varying from near the sea-level up to about 2,000 feet in height. The following table contains the principal species, the places where grown, and the commercial name : —

Botanical Name.	Where Grown.	Commercial Name.
Theobroma angustifolia .	Mexico.	
T. bicolor . .	Brazil . . .	{ Maranhan. { Bahia.
	New Granada,	Magdalena.
T. Cacao (sativa)	Australia, Bourbon, Ceylon, Cuba, Dominico, Guadaloupe,	The name of each country.
	Guatemala . .	Central American.
	Guinea . . .	African.
	Hayti, India, Jamaica, Java, Madagascar, Martinique, Mauritius, Philippines, St. Croix, St. Lucia, St. Vincent, Trinidad,	The name of each country.

Botanical Name.	Where Grown.	Commercial Name.
T. Cacao (sati-va.)	Venezuela .	Maracaibo. Caracas.
T. glauca.		
T. Guyanensis,	Cayenne . .	Berbice.
	Surinam. . .	Surinam.
T. microcarpa,	Ecuador . .	Esmeralda.
	Peru . . .	Guayaquil.
T. ovalifolia .	Mexico . . .	Soconusco.
T. speciosa . .	Brazil . . .	Para.
T. sylvestris .	Brazil . . .	
	Jamaïca . . .	

Besides the above-mentioned species, distinguished by botanists, *T. Cacao*, which is the most widely and largely cultivated, is divided by cocoa-planters into several varieties, the differences observed being due to the long-continued influences of varied climates, soils and modes of culture. The best of these is the Creole (or *Criollo* of the Spanish inhabitants of South America). The pods are small; but the nuts are thick, short, and almost globular, pale crimson in color, and of slightly bitter but agreeable flavor. This variety is

becoming scarce, chiefly through the bad
policy of replacing decayed trees by in-
ferior specimens. The next variety is the
Forastero, the best kinds of which are the
Cundeamar, of two descriptions, one with
yellow, the other with red pods. The
former is the better, containing large seeds
which, in color and the ease with which
they are fermented, resemble the *Criollo*.
The third variety is the *Amelonado;* and
the fourth and lowest is the *Calabacillo*,
whose seeds are small, bitter, and of a dark
crimson color.

All the varieties except the *Criollo*,
which is probably confined to Venezuela,
are known collectively as *Trinitario*, or
" Trinidad," — the best being but little in-
ferior to *Criollo* in the matter of quality,
and superior on the score of fruitfulness.
Hence Trinidad forms the principal nursery
from which plants or seeds are procured
for new plantations.

The various kinds of cocoa may be

placed in about the following order of merit: Soconusco (Mexico) and Esmeralda, (Ecuador), mostly, it is said, consumed at home ; Caracas and Puerto Cabello (Venezuela) ; Trinitario ; Magdalena and Carthagena, New Granada ; Para ; Bahia.[1]

The British West Indies appear to take the lead among the producers for exportation ; Ecuador stands second, Venezuela third, and Brazil fourth. The larger part of the Brazilian crop goes to France ; and the larger part of the Ecuadorian to Spain.

A French officer who served in the West Indies for a period of fifteen years, during the early part of the last century, wrote, as the result of his personal observations, a treatise on "The Natural History of Chocolate, being a distinct and particular Account of the Cacao-Tree, its Growth and Culture,

---

[1] Spon's Encyclopædia, etc., Div. II.

and the Preparation, Excellent Properties, and Medicinal Virtues of its Fruit," which received the approbation of the Regent of the Faculty of Medicine at Paris, and which was translated and published in London in 1730.

From this rare and valuable little work the following extracts are made : —

"The cacao-tree almost all the year bears fruit of all ages, which ripens successively, but never grows on the end of little branches, as our fruits in Europe do, but along the trunk and chief boughs, which is not rare in these countries, where several trees do the like.   Such an unusual appearance would seem strange in the eyes of Europeans, who have never seen anything of that kind ; but, if one examines the matter a little, the philosophical reason of this disposition is very obvious.   One may easily apprehend that if nature had placed such bulky fruit at the ends of the branches their great weight must necessarily break them, and the fruit would fall before it came to maturity.

"The fruit is contained in a husk, or shell, which, from an exceedingly small beginning, attains in the space of four months to the bigness and shape of a cucumber. The lower end is sharp, and furrowed lengthwise like a melon. This shell in the first months is either red or white, or a mixture of red and yellow. This variety of colors makes three sorts of cacao-trees, which have nothing else to distinguish them but this. . . . If one cleaves one of these shells lengthways it will appear almost half an inch thick, and its capacity full of chocolate kernels, the intervals of which, before they are ripe, are filled with a hard white substance, which at length turns into a mucilage of a very grateful acidity. For this reason it is common for people to take some of the kernels with their covers and hold them in their mouths, which is mighty refreshing, and proper to quench thirst.

But they take heed of biting them, because the films of the kernels are extremely bitter.

" When one nicely examines the inward structure of these shells, and anatomizes, as it were, all their parts, one shall find that the fibres of the stalk of the fruit passing through the shell are divided into five branches ; that each of these branches is subdivided into several filaments, every one of which terminates at the larger end of these kernels, and altogether resembles a bunch of grapes, containing from twenty to thirty-five single ones, or more, ranged and placed in an admirable order. When one takes off the film that covers one of the kernels the substance of it appears, which is tender, smooth, and inclining to violet color, and is seemingly divided into several lobes, though in reality they are but two ; but very irregular and difficult to be disengaged from each other."

An interesting supplement to this description of the product in the West Indies, written more than a century and a half ago, will be found in the following report, made last year to the State Department at Washington, by the U.S. Consul at La Guayra, in relation to the cultivation of cocoa in Venezuela, where the choicest variety of the exported product, the Caracas, is raised : —

" The tree grows to the average height of thirteen feet, and from five to eight inches in diameter, is of spreading habit and healthy growth, and, although requiring much more care and attention than the coffee-tree, yet its equally reliable crops require comparatively little labor in properly preparing for the market.

". . . There are two varieties of the cocoa-tree cultivated in Venezuela, known as El Criollo and El Trinitario, respectively, the former of which, though not so prolific nor as early fruiting as the latter, is yet superior to it in size, color, sweetness, and oleaginous properties of the fruit, and in the fact that it always finds ready sale, while the latter is often dull or neglected. The difference in price of the two varieties is also marked, the former being quoted at $28 to $30 per fanega (110 pounds), while the latter commands approximately half that price.

" While coffee can be successfully cultivated under a temperature of 60 degrees F., the cocoa-tree, for proper development and remunerative crops, requires a temperature of 80 degrees F. ; hence the area of the cocoa belt is comparatively restricted, and the cocoa-planter presumably has not to fear the fierce competition that he has encountered in the cultivation of cotton and coffee. Besides the condition of temperature above stated, this crop needs a moist soil and humid atmosphere, and so the lands along the coast of the Caribbean sea, sloping from the mountain-tops to the shore, bedewed by the exhalations of the sea and irrigated by the numerous rivulets that course down the valleys, are found to be, in all respects, well adapted to the profitable cultivation of cocoa. And while the lands in the interior possessing facilities for irrigation may be said to be equally as good for the purpose, yet the absence of roads, and the consequently difficult transportation of produce on the backs of donkeys over rugged mountain paths, materially reduce the profits on the crop before it reaches the market.

" A cocoa plantation is set in quite the same manner as an apple-orchard, except that the young stalks may be transplanted from the nursery after two months' growth. No preparation of the soil is deemed necessary, and no manures are applied. The young trees are planted about fifteen feet equidistant, which will accommodate two hundred trees to the acre. Between rows, and at like spaces, are planted rows of the

Bucare, a tree of rapid growth, that serves to shade the soil as well as to shield the young trees from the torrid sun. Small permanent trenches must be maintained from tree to tree throughout the entire length of the rows, so that, at least once in the week, the stream, descending from the mountains, may be turned into these little channels and bear needful moisture to trees and soil. At the age of five years the plantation begins to bear fruit, and annually yields two crops, that ripening in June being termed the crop of San Juan, and that maturing at Christmas being known as the crop of La Navidad. The average age to which the trees attain, under proper care, may be estimated at forty years, during which period it will give fair to full crops of fruit; but of course it must be understood that, as in our fruit-orchards, a new tree must be set from time to time to replace one that may be decayed or blighted. After careful inquiry it may be safely stated that the average crop of the cocoa plantation at ten years of age, and under a proper state of cultivation, will amount to five hundred or six hundred pounds per acre.

" The fruit or seed of the cocoa, in form, size, and color, is quite similar to the almond. These seeds, to the number of sixty or eighty,[1] are encased in a pod,

[1] This statement is incorrect. The average number is about twenty-five; the maximum number would not exceed forty. It is curious to note the different statements of those who are regarded as authorities on the subject. Dampier ("A New Voyage round the World") says there are commonly near a hundred; Thomas Gage ("New Survey of the West Indies ") says there are from thirty to forty; Colmenero ("A Curious Discourse upon Chocolate") says ten or twelve; Oexmelin ("The History of Adventures") says ten to fourteen. The French officer, in his "Natural History of Chocolate," says (and says truly), " I can affirm, after a thousand trials, that I never found more nor less than twenty-five. Perhaps, if one were to seek out the largest shells in the most fruitful soil and growing on the most flourishing trees, one might find forty kernels; but as it is not likely one would ever meet with more, so, on the other hand, it is not probable one would ever find less than fifteen except they are abortive, or the fruit of a tree worn out with age in a barren soil, or without culture."

which, except in color, is the counterpart of a young muskmelon, being elongated and ribbed in the same manner. Its color, when green, is like that of the egg-plant, but, on ripening, it assumes a reddish hue. A peculiarity of the cocoa is that it bears fruit " from the ground up," the trunk yielding fruit as well as the branches. Upon ripening, the pods are gathered from the trees and heaped in piles on the ground, where they are left for some days to ferment, after which they burst open, when the seed must be shelled out. After a light exposure to the sun, during which time great care must be taken to protect them from the rain, they are sacked and ready for market.

" The cocoa-trees, when very young, require to be carefully watched, to protect them from the ravages of the borers, which, instead of entering the trees near the ground or in the roots, as is the case with the borers in our peach-orchards, burrow under

the bark of the trunk and girdle the trees.
After a few years of care all danger from
this source is removed. The only disease
to which the tree is subject is *la mancha*,
which is an affection similar to the pear
blight in the United States, though not so
obstinate and fatal, and which, by promptly
cutting away the diseased bark, may be
usually arrested. The squirrels and wood-
peckers also must be guarded against, as
they are very fond of the young fruit. It
happens too, though rarely, that a period
of ten or twelve days of continuous rainy
and cloudy weather ensues, in which event
much of the fruit is blighted and falls from
the trees. These, it is believed, comprise
all the casualties to which the tree and the
green crop are exposed; but which, when
compared with the usual contingencies that
affect our own orchards and fruit crops,
may not be considered more damaging or
discouraging.

"In the tillage of the soil and the econo-

mies of agriculture the people of Venezuela are probably not in advance of those
who scratched and scraped the earth before
the deluge. A people that will plough
with a forked stick, and plant corn with an
iron crow-bar, as is practised here, have
much to learn in respect to the laws of
nature and the appliances of art. And
the resultant idea, on a practical review of
the subject, is that, if a fair amount of
intelligent industry and care could be in-
vested in the cultivation of this crop, it
would undoubtedly yield a surprisingly
satisfactory percentage of remunerative
returns."

The method of preparing the fruit for
shipment is thus described in the recent edition of the " Encyclopædia Britannica " : —
" In gathering, the workman is careful
to cut down only fully ripened pods, which
he adroitly accomplishes with a long pole
armed with two prongs, or a knife at its

extremity. The pods are left in a heap on the ground for about twenty-four hours; they are then cut open and the seeds are taken out and carried in baskets to the place where they undergo the operation of sweating or curing. There the acid juice which accompanies the seeds is first drained off, after which they are placed in a sweating-box, in which they are enclosed and allowed to ferment for some time, great care being taken to keep the temperature from rising too high. The fermenting process is, in some cases, affected by throwing the seeds into holes or trenches in the ground and covering them with earth or clay. The seeds in this process, which is called claying, are occasionally stirred to keep the fermentation from proceeding too violently. The sweating is a process which requires the very greatest attention and experience, as on it, to a great extent, depends the flavor of the seeds and their fitness for preservation. The operation varies according to the state of the weather, but a period of about two days yields the best results. Thereafter the seeds are exposed to the sun for drying, and those of a fine quality should then assume a warm, reddish tint, which characterizes beans of a superior quality."

The shell of the nut is prolonged in the form of thin septa into the inner part of the seed. The relative proportions of shell and nib are approximately as 1 : 8, the nib being much the more abundant. They vary considerably in size. Single seeds may be picked out which weigh as much as 2.7 grammes;[1] but the average weight is much less, viz., 1.2 grammes.

The following determinations of the weights of the different kinds of seeds were made by J. Alfred Wanklyn, the well-known analyst:—

---

[1] A gramme is equal to 15.432 English grains.

Name of Cocoa.	Weight of 100 Nuts. Grammes.
Common Trinidad	98.
Fair, good Trinidad	123.2
Very fine Trinidad	178.7
Medium Granada	104.5
Fine Granada	131.
Caracas	130.3
Dominican	110.
Fine Surinam	122.
Fine Surinam (small)	71.5
Bahia (Brazil)	118.
Mexican	136.5
African	128.

The nut, in its unprepared condition,
is not an article of retail trade. Before
it reaches the consumer it requires much
preparation, and without such preparation
it is in as impracticable a condition as
unground grain before the miller has converted it into flour.

III.

EARLY USE.

THE name chocolate is nearly the same
in most European languages, and is
taken from the Mexican name of the
drink, chocolatl, or cacahuatl. *Atl* is
common enough in Mexican words, and
is known to signify water. What the first
part of the word means is not so clear. A
French writer says it signifies noise; and
that the drink was so named because it was
beaten to a froth before being drunk.

The Spaniards found chocolate in common use among the Mexicans at the time
of the invasion under Cortez, in 1519, and
it was introduced into Spain immediately
after. The Mexicans not only used chocolate as a staple article of food, but they used
the seeds of the cacao-tree as a medium

of exchange. An early writer says, "In certain provinces called Guatimala and Soconusco there is growing a great store of cacao, which is a berry like unto an almond. It is the best merchandise that is in all the Indies. The Indians make drink of it, and in like manner meat to eat. It goeth currently for money in any market, or fair, and may buy flesh, fish, bread or cheese, or other things."

In the "True History of the Conquest of Mexico," by Bernal Diaz, an officer under Cortez, it is related that "from time to time a liquor prepared from cocoa and of a stimulating or corroborative quality, as we are told, was presented to Montezuma in a golden cup. We could not at the time see if he drank it or not, but I observed a number of jars — above fifty — brought in and filled with foaming chocolate."

Thomas Gage, in his "New Survey of

the West Indies," first published in 1648, gives the following interesting account of the Spanish and Indian way of making and drinking chocolate some two hundred and fifty years ago : —

"Now, for the making or compounding of this drink, I shall set down here the method. The cacao and the other ingredients must be beaten in a mortar of stone, or (as the Indians use) ground upon a broad stone, which they call *Metate*, and is only made for that use. But first the ingredients are all to be dried, except the *Achiotte* (annotto), with care that they be beaten to powder, keeping them still in stirring that they be not burnt, or become black ; for if they be overdried they will be bitter and lose their virtue. The cinnamon and the long red pepper are to be first beaten with the anniseed, and then the cacao, which must be beaten by little and little till it be all powdered, and in the beating it must be turned round that it may

mix the better. Every one of these ingredients must be beaten by itself, and then all be
put into the vessel where the cacao is,
which you must stir together with a spoon,
and then take out that paste, and put it
into the mortar, under which there must
be a little fire, after the confection is made ;
but if more fire be put under than will only
warm it, then the unctuous part will dry
away. The *Achiotte* also must be put in
in the beating, that it may the better take
the colour. All the ingredients must be
searced, save only the cacao, and if from
the cacao the dry shell be taken, it will be
the better. When it is well beaten and incorporated (which will be known by the
shortnesse of it) then with a spoon (so in
the Indias is used) is taken up some of the
paste, which will be almost liquid, and
made into tablets, or else without a spoon
put into boxes, and when it is cold it will
be hard.

" Those that make it into tablets put a

spoonful of the paste upon a piece of
paper (the Indians put it upon the leaf of
a plaintain tree), where, being put into
the shade (for in the sun it melts and dis-
solves), it grows hard ; and then bowing
the paper or leaf, the tablet fals off by
reason of the fatnesse of the paste.   But if
it be put into anything of earth or wood, it
stickes fast, and will not come off but with
scraping or breaking.   The manner of
drinking it is divers ; the one (being the
way most used in Mexico) is to take it
hot with Atolle, dissolving a tablet in hot
water, and stirring and beating it in the
cup, when it is to be drunk, with a Molinet, and when it is well stirred to a scumme
or froth, then to fill the cup with hot
Atolle, and so drink it sup by sup.   Another way is that the chocolate, being dissolved with cold water and stirred with the
Molinet, and the scumme being taken off
and put into another vessel, the remainder
be set upon the fire, with as much sugar

as will sweeten it, and when it is warme,
then to powre it upon the scumme which
was taken off before, and so to drink it.
But the most ordinary way is to warme the
water very hot, and then to powre out
half the cup full that you mean to drink;
and to put into it a tablet or two, or as
much as will thicken reasonably the water,
and then grinde it well with the Molinet,
and when it is well ground and risen to a
scumme, to fill the cup with hot water, and
so drink it by sups (having sweetened it
with sugar), and to eat it with a little con-
serve or maple bred, steeped into the
chocolatte.

" Besides these ways there is another way
(which is much used in the Island of Santo
Domingo), which is to put the chocolatte
into a pipkin with a little water, and to let
it boyle well till it be dissolved, and then
to put in sufficient water and sugar according to the quantity of the chocolatte, and
then to boyle it again untill there comes

an oily scumme upon it, and then to drink
it.

"There is another way yet to drink chocolatte, which is cold, which the Indians use
at feasts to refresh themselves, and it is
made after this manner: The chocolatte
(which is made with none, or very few,
ingredients) being dissolved in cold water
with the Molinet, they take off the scumme
or crassy part, which riseth in great quantity, especially when the cacao is older and
more putrefied. The scumme they lay aside
in a little dish by itself, and then put sugar
into that part from whence was taken the
scumme, and then powre it from on high
into the scumme, and so drink it cold.
And this drink is so cold that it agreeth
not with all men's stomachs; for by experience it hath been found that it doth .
hurt by causing pains in the stomach, especially to women.

"The third way of taking it is the most
used, and thus certainly it doth no hurt,

neither know I why it may not be used as
well in England as in other parts, both
hot and cold; for where it is so much used,
the most, if not all, as well in the Indias
as in Spain, Italy, Flanders (which is a
cold countrey), find that it agreeth well with
them. True it is, it is used more in the
Indias than in the European parts, because
there the stomachs are more apt to faint
than here, and a cup of chocolatte well
confectioned comforts and strengthens the
stomach. For myself I must say, I used
it twelve years constantly, drinking one
cup in the morning, another yet before
dinner between nine or ten of the clock;
another within an hour or two after dinner,
and another between four and five in the
afternoon; and when I was purposed to
sit up late to study, I would take another
cup about seven or eight at night, which
would keep me waking till about midnight.
And if by chance I did neglect any of
these accustomed houres, I presently found

my stomach fainty. And with this custome
I lived twelve years in those parts healthy,
without any obstructions, or oppilations,
not knowing what either ague or feaver
was."

M. Ferdinand Denis, in " La Legende
du Cacahuatl," makes the following interesting statement in regard to the preparation of chocolate in ancient Mexico : —

" Torquemada, the learned historian,
and Thomas Gage, the conscientious trav-
eller, agree in telling us that *hot* chocolate
was an invention of the Castilians. The
first of these writers, who lived at the end
of the sixteenth century, says so positively ;
in his time it had been used for only a few
years.

" Would you know now what chocolate
was when the learned Antonio Colmenero
de Ledesma gave his receipt? I copy it for
you here : —

" ' Take a hundred cacao kernels, two

heads of Chili or long peppers, a handful
of anise or orjevala, and two of mesachusil
or vanilla, — or, instead, six Alexandria
roses, powdered, — two drachms of cinnamon, a dozen almonds and as many hazel-
nuts, a half pound of white sugar, and
annotto enough to color it, and you have the
king of chocolates.'

" I must say a word concerning another
substance allied to the chocolate, beloved
of the Americans. I speak of *atola*, which
has been handed down to us. There was
the *atola* of dry and of green maize ; the
latter was served on elegant tables. Composed of maize in the milky stage, sweetened with the vegetable honey of the agave,
sometimes, also, flavored with excellent
vanilla, it had the appearance of blanc-
mange. On this mixture was poured chocolate prepared cold. It can be understood
how the most delicate palates could relish
it. I say nothing here of the coarse
mixtures of dry flour, or *frisoles*, which

were mixed with the cacao; it was a
vulgar food, endurable only by the common people.

"Not to leave too incomplete this sketch
of various antiquities, often examined, but
still obscure, I must touch upon the still
less familiar subject of American ceramics,
which will not be the least curious para-
graph. The Mexicans had vases specially
set apart for beverages of the most varied
description, which were served at their festivals, from the ordinary pulque to the most
delicate octli. There were among them,
without doubt, chocolate pots of great
value. The historian of King Tezozomoc
leaves us no doubt on this subject. He
names, it is true, a series of ornamented
vases without making us acquainted with
their special use; but he is much more ex-
plicit when he speaks of a cup, ready made
by nature, but which the goldsmith's art
had covered with the most elegant orna-
ments. Thanks to him, we know that

cocoa was offered to distinguished person-
ages in a tortoise shell, highly polished and
ornamented with gold arabesques. And it
was very probably in this manner that Fer-
nando Cortez drank his first chocolate."

The Spaniards thus early acquired a
knowledge of the fruit and of the manner
of preparing it, which they kept secret for
many years, selling it very profitably as
chocollat to the wealthy and luxurious
classes of Europe. But it was, as already
stated, an expensive preparation, and did
not come into use until long after the public
coffee-houses of London were established.

Says Brillat-Savarin, in his famous "Physiologie du Gout," "Chocolate came over
the mountains [from Spain to France] with
Anne of Austria, daughter of Philip III.,
and Queen of Louis XIII. The Spanish
monks also spread the knowledge of it by
the presents they made to their brothers in
France. The various ambassadors of Spain

also contributed to bring it into fashion;
and at the beginning of the Regency it
was more universally in use than coffee,
inasmuch as it was taken as an agreeable
article of food, while coffee still passed
only for a beverage of luxury and a curios-
ity.   It is well known that Linnæus called
the fruit of the cocoa-tree *theobroma* ' food
for the gods.'   The cause of this emphatic
qualification has been sought, and attributed
by some to the fact that he was extrava-
gantly fond of chocolate; by others to his
desire to please his confessor; and by
others to his gallantry, a queen having first
introduced it into France."

The Spanish ladies of the New World, it
is said, carry their love for chocolate to such
a degree that, not content with partaking of it
several times a day, they have it sometimes
carried after them to church.   This favor-
ing of the senses often drew upon them the
censures of the bishop; but the Reverend
Father Escobar, whose metaphysics were as

subtle as his morality was accommodating, declared, formally, that a fast was not broken by chocolate prepared with water; thus wire-drawing, in favor of his penitents, the ancient adage: "*Liquidum non frangit je junium.*"

The earliest intimation of the introduction of cocoa into England is found in an announcement in the *Public Advertiser* of Tuesday, 16th June, 1657 (more than a hundred and thirty years after its introduction into Spain), stating that "in Bishopsgate street, in Queen's Head alley, at a Frenchman's house, is an excellent West India drink, called chocolate, to be sold, where you may have it ready at any time; and also unmade, at reasonable rates."

Two years later, in the *Mercurius Politicus* for June, 1659, it is stated that "Chocolate, an excellent West India drink, is sold in Queen's Head alley, in Bishopsgate street, by a Frenchman who did formerly sell it in Grace Church street, and Clement's Churchyard, being the first man who did sell it in England; and its virtues are highly extolled."

A book written in the time of Charles II., entitled "The Indian Nectar, or a Discourse concerning Chocolate, etc.," says the best kind can be purchased of one Mortimer, "an honest though poor man, living in East Smithfield," for 6s. 8d. per pound, and commoner sorts for about half that price.

About the beginning of the eighteenth century chocolate had become an exceedingly fashionable beverage, and the cocoa-tree was a favorite sign and name for places of public refreshment. Cocoa and chocolate are frequently mentioned in contemporary literature; and among others Pope, in his "Rape of the Lock," alludes to it; the negligent spirit, fixed like Ixion, —

> "In fumes of burning chocolate shall glow,
> And tremble at the sea that froths below."

Down to a late period (1832) the consumption of cocoa in England was confined
within very narrow limits, owing to the
oppressiveness of the duties with which it
was loaded. The ruin of the cocoa plantations which once flourished in Jamaica
was caused, says Mr. Bryan Edwards, the
historian, by the heavy hand of ministerial
exaction. In 1832 the duty on cocoa from
a British possession was reduced from 6d.
to 2d. per pound. The result was that the
consumption which, during the three years
ending in 1831, averaged only 440,578
pounds a year, shortly increased to an
average of 2,072,335 pounds. The duty of
6d. per pound on foreign cocoa was continued some time longer; but in 1853 the
duties were finally equalized and fixed at
1d. per pound, and on paste or chocolate
at 2d. The duties on husks and shells
were reduced to 2s. per cwt. in 1855.

It is stated, on what appears to be good

authority,[1] that the chocolate-mill erected on Neponset river, in the town of Dorchester, Mass, in 1765, was the first mill of that kind established in the British provinces of North America. It was connected with a saw-mill, operated by water-power, and was regarded as a somewhat doubtful experiment. Its establishment was due to the representations made by John Hannan, an Irish immigrant, who had learned the business of chocolate-making in England. The new industry prospered in a small way, and on the death of Hannan, in 1780, Dr. James Baker established the house which has continued the business without interruption from that day to this.

In the early days the crude cocoa was brought to the American market by the Massachusetts traders, who received it in exchange for the fish and other articles which they shipped to the West Indies and

---

[1] History of the town of Dorchester, Mass., 1857.

Central and South America ; and the direct
connection with the producers, thus early
established, has ever since been maintained.

In giving an account of the manufactures in Boston, in 1794, J. L. Bishop, in
his " History of American Manufactures,"
says : " Chocolate had been long made
from the large quantities of cocoa obtained
in the West India trade, and had been
greatly expedited by recent inventions.
The chocolate-mill of Mr. Welsh, at the
North End, could turn out 2,500 cwt.
daily."

It is a curious fact that on the spot where
the industry was first started, nearly a
century and a quarter ago, the business has
continued and attained the highest development. From the small beginning by Dr.
Baker there has grown up one of the
greatest establishments in the world, — the
house of Walter Baker & Co., — an establishment which competes successfully for
prizes in all the great industrial exhibitions

of the world, whose influence is felt in the
great commercial centres, and whose pros-
perity promotes the welfare of men who
labor under a tropical sun in the cultivation of one of the choicest fruits of the
earth.

IV.

PROPERTIES, ETC.

THE most thorough and comprehensive analysis of the properties of cocoa is given by J. Alfred Wanklyn, in " A Practical Treatise on the Analysis of Tea, Coffee, Cocoa, Chocolate, etc.," published in London, in 1874. The following table gives the results obtained by the leading authorities : —

	Lampadius.	Payen.	Johnson.	Playfair and Lankester.	Boussingault.	Mitscherlich.	Average of several other Analyses.
Fat (Cocoa-Butter)	53.10	52.00	51.00	50.00	44.00	45.00	50.00
Albuminoid Substances	18.70			20.00		13.00	18.00
Albumin		} 20.00			20.00		
Fibrin			20.00				
Gluten							
Extractive Matter						0.60	
Sugar	10.91	10.00	} 22.00	7.00			10.00
Starch	7.75			6.00		14.00	8.00
Gum	0.90				6.00		
Lignine					} 13.00		
Cellulose		2.00		4.00		6.08	2.60
Woody Fibre	2.01	traces		2.00		3.05	6.00
Coloring Matter	5.20	10.00		5.00		5.06	1.50
Water			5.00	2.00	11.00	1.02	
Theobromine		2.00	2.00	4.00	2.00		
Salts		4.00			4.00		
Ash						3.05	3.60
Humic Acid	1.43						0.30
Parts unaccounted for						9.14	
Total	100.00	100.00	100.00	100.00	100.00	100.00	100.00

" The most abundant constituent of the seed," says Wanklyn, " is the fat, or cocoa-butter, which constitutes about one-half of the entire seed. Owing, no doubt, to this circumstance, the specific gravity of the seeds is less than unity, and they float on water. After being kept for some days in contact with the water some of the fat makes its escape, and the seeds sink to the bottom.

" I attach great importance to the determination of the ash. The following determinations of ash have been recently made in my laboratory : —

	Percentage of Ash.
Common Trinidad	3.37
Very fine Trinidad	3.62
Fair, good, fine Trinidad . . .	3.64
Fine Granada	3.12
Medium Granada	3.06
Caracas	4.58
Bahia (Brazil)	3.31

	Percentage of Ash.
Fine Surinam	3.06
Fine Surinam (small)	3.15
Mexican	4.27
Dominican	2.82
African	2.68
The mean of the twelve being .	3.39

" Separate determinations of the ash of the nib and the shell have also been made. In the nib of the Caracas the ash amounted to 3.95 per cent., whereof 2.00 was soluble in water, and 1.95 insoluble in water.

" In the nib of the Mexican seeds the ash was found to be 2.59 per cent., whereof 0.89 was soluble, and 1.70 insoluble, in water. The shell (which, as mentioned above, formed only a very small portion of the entire seed) is much richer in mineral matter or ash. I have found as much as 7.81 per cent. of ash in the shell. The composition of the ash of the shell is very different from that of the nib ; whilst the ash of the shell is rich in carbonates that of the nib is almost devoid of carbonates.

" A very careful analysis of the ash of the entire seed has been recently made by my friend, Mr. Wm. Bettel, in my laboratory. The results are as follows : —

" Composition of ash of the entire seeds (Caracas), —

Potash $K_2 O$	29.81
Chloride of Sodium Na Cl . .	6.10
Peroxide of Iron $Fi_2 O_3$ . . .	1.60
Alumina $Al_2 O_3$	2.40
Lime Ca O	7.72
Magnesia Mg O	7.90
Phosphoric Acid $P_2 O_5$ . . .	24.28
Sulphuric Acid S O_3	1.92
Carbonic Acid C O_2	0.98
Silica Si O_2	5.00
Sand	12.15
	———
	99.86

" From this analysis it is apparent that the main constituent of the ash is phosphate of potash, and that there is almost total absence of carbonates. The ash of the shell being, as has been said, highly charged with carbonates, it follows that, in obtaining the ash of the entire seed, we cause the phosphates of the nib to decompose the carbonates of the shell, and so obtain an ash devoid of carbonates.

" The large proportion of phosphate of potash in cocoa (certainly not far from one per cent. in the seed of good quality) is worthy the attention of the physician, and no doubt gives an especial value to a dietary consisting largely of cocoa. It will further be observed that the fine kinds of cocoa-seeds are rich in phosphate of potash. . . . .

" Mixtures of cocoa with starch and sugar have long been perfectly legitimate, provided no deception as to the strength in cocoa be practised."

In conclusion he says : " The preparations of cocoa constitute food rather than drink, being highly nutritious in every sense of the term. The fat present in cocoa — viz., the cocoa-butter — appears to be of a particularly available description. It is said never to become rancid, and merits an elaborate examination. Whether it be owing to peculiarities in the fat of cocoa, or whether it be the theobromine that is particularly efficient, certain it is that cocoa will sometimes nourish when nothing else will, and cocoa is occasionally invaluable to the physician."

V.

VALUE AS FOOD.

DR. EDWARD SMITH, LL.B., F.R.S., in his valuable work on "Foods," for the International Scientific Series, says:—

"These well-known substances (cocoa and chocolate) are valuable foods, since they are not only allied to tea and coffee as respiratory excitants, but possess a large quantity of fat and other food materials. . . .

"The following is the analysis of the cocoa-bean, from various localities, by Tuchen:—

	Surinam.	Caracas.	Para.	Trinidad.
Theobromine, per. ct.	0.56	0.55	0.66	0.48
Cocoa, red . . .	6.61	6.18	6.18	6.22
Cocoa-butter . . .	36.97	35.08	34.48	36.42

	Surinam.	Caracas.	Para.	Trinidad.
Gluten	3.20	3.21	2.99	3.15
Starch	0.55	0.62	0.28	0.51
Gum	0.69	1.19	0.78	0.61
Extractive matter .	4.14	6.22	6.02	5.48
Humic acid . . .	7.25	9.28	8.63	9.25
Cellulose	30.00	28.66	30.21	29.86
Salts	3.00	2.91	3.00	2.98
Water	6.01	5.58	5.55	4.88

" This substance," he goes on to say, " in its action is less exciting to the nervous system than tea or coffee, and at the same time it contains a much larger proportion of nutritive material. Moreover, its flavor is not lessened by the addition of milk, so that it can be boiled in milk only, and thus produce a most agreeable and nutritious food. There are, therefore, many persons, states of system and circumstances, in which its use is to be preferred to either tea or coffee."

A writer in Blackwood's Magazine (1854, V. 75) says: "Of all the varieties of ordinary human food cocoa has the closest resemblance to milk;" and he gives the following analyses of dried milk and the dried kernel of the cocoa-bean: —

	Cocoa-Beans.	Dried Milk.
Gluten or Caseine	18	35
Starch or Sugar	23	37
Fat	55	24
Mineral matter	4	4

"These numbers show," he says, "that the bean is rich in all the important nutritious principles which are found to coexist in our most valued forms of ordinary food. It differs from milk chiefly in the larger proportion of fat it contains, and hence it cannot be used so largely without admixture as the more familiar milk. When mixed with water, however, it is more properly compared with milk than with

the infusions of little direct nutritive
value, like those of tea and coffee ; and, on
the other hand, it has the great advantage
over milk, over beef-tea, and other similar
beverages, that it contains the substance
theobromine and the volatile empyrematic
oil, — both possessed of very valuable
properties. Thus it unites in itself the
exhilarating and other special qualities
which distinguish tea, with the strengthening and ordinary body-supporting qualities
of milk."

Brillat-Savarin, from whose work we
have already quoted, says : —

" Chocolate has given rise to profound
dissertations, whose object has been to determine its nature and properties, and to
place it in the category of hot, cold, or
temperate foods ; and it must be confessed
that these learned writings have contributed
but very slightly to the demonstration of
the truth.

" But it was left for those two great mas-
ters, time and experience, to decide that
chocolate, carefully prepared, is an article
of food as wholesome as it is agreeable;
that it is nourishing, easy of digestion, and
does not possess those qualities injurious to
beauty with which coffee has been re-
proached; that it is excellently adapted to
persons who are obliged to a great concen-
tration of intellect in the toils of the pulpit
or the bar, and especially to travellers;
that it suits the most feeble stomach; that
excellent effects have been produced by it
in chronic complaints, and that it is a last
resource in affections of the pylorus.

" The various properties are due to the
fact that, chocolate being, strictly speak-
ing, only an elæosaccharum (oil of sugar),
there are few substances which contain
in an equal volume more nourishing particles, — the consequence being that it is
almost entirely assimilated.

" During the war (of the Spanish Suc-

cession) cocoa was scarce, and very dear.
It was attempted to find a substitute, but
all efforts were in vain; and one of the
greatest benefits of the peace was the re-
lieving us of the various brews, which it
was necessary to taste out of politeness,
but which were no more like chocolate
than the infusion of chiccory was like
Mocha coffee.

" Some persons complain of being unable
to digest chocolate ; others, on the contrary, pretend that it has not sufficient
nourishment, and that the effect disappears
too soon. It is probable that the former
have only themselves to blame, and that
the chocolate which they use is of bad
quality or badly made ; for good and well-
made chocolate must suit every stomach
which retains the slightest digestive power.

" In regard to the others the remedy is
an easy one ; they should reënforce their
breakfast with a *paté*, a cutlet, or a kid-
ney ; moisten the whole with a good

draught of soconusco chocolate, and thank God for a stomach of such superior activity.

" This gives me an opportunity to make an observation whose accuracy may be depended upon.

" After a good, complete and copious breakfast, if we take in addition a cup of well-made chocolate, digestion will be perfectly accomplished in three hours, and we may dine whenever we like. Out of zeal for science, and by dint of eloquence, I have induced many ladies to try this experiment. They all declared, in the beginning, that it would kill them; but they have all thriven on it, and have not failed to glorify their teacher.

" The people who make constant use of chocolate are the ones who enjoy the most steady health, and are the least subject to a multitude of little ailments which destroy the comfort of life; their plumpness is also more equal. These are two advantages which every one may verify among his own friends, and wherever the practice is in use.

" This is the place to speak of the properties of chocolate with amber, — properties which I have proved with many experiments, and the results of which I am proud to offer to my readers.

" Let every man, then, who has drunk too deep of the cup of pleasure ; every man who has spent in work the time which should be devoted to sleep ; every man of wit who feels himself temporarily growing stupid ; every man who finds the air damp, the time long, and the atmosphere difficult to endure ; every man who is tormented with a fixed idea which takes away from him the liberty of thought, — let all these, I say, administer to themselves a good half-litre of amber chocolate, in the proportion of sixty or seventy grains of amber to the pound, and they will see wonders.

"In my particular way of specifying things I call amber chocolate *chocolate for the afflicted*, because each one of these various conditions which I have designated has something in common which resembles affliction."

M. Boussingault,[1] a member of the French Institute, in an interesting paper printed in the "*Annales de Physique et du Chimie*," says : —

"Chocolate contains a very large proportion of nutritive matter in a small volume. In an expedition to a great distance, where it is imperatively necessary to reduce the weight of the rations, chocolate offers undeniable advantages, as I have had frequent occasions to notice. Humboldt recalls what has been said with reason, that in Africa rice, gum, and

---

[1] Jean Baptiste Joseph Dieudonné Boussingault, French chemist, served in his youth on the staff of Bolivar, the liberator of South America.

butter enable men to cross the desert; and he adds that, in the New World, chocolate and corn-meal render the plateaus of the Andes, and the vast, uninhabited forests, accessible to man.

"In Central America, when they organize a river expedition, or traverse the forests, they prepare chocolate for provision with eighty parts of cocoa to twenty of coarse sugar, the composition being as follows: —

Sugar	200
Butter	410
Albumen	100
Phosphates and salts	30
Other matter	260
	1,000

" Each man receives 60 grammes (about 2 ounces) of this chocolate per day, in which there are 12 grammes of sugar, 26 of butter,

and 6 of albumen. It is a useful addition
to the ration formed of beef slightly salted
and dried in the air, of rice, of corn biscuit, or of cassava muffins.

" The infusion of tea, mate (Paraguay
tea), and coffee are not, of course, to be considered as food. The amount of solid
matter in them is very slight, and their
effects are due only to their alkaloids.

" This is not true of chocolate, which is
at the same time complete food and an
active excitant, since it approaches in composition that model food, milk. In fact
we have seen that in cocoa there is legu-
mine and albumen, associated with fat,
sugar to sustain respiratory combustion,
phosphates, which are the basis of the
bones, and — what milk does not have
— theobromine and a delicate aroma.
Roasted, ground and mixed with sugar,
cocoa becomes chocolate, the nutritive
properties of which astonished the Spanish
soldiers that invaded Mexico."

A competent writer, in the last edition of the " Encyclopædia Britannica," says : —

" The constitution upon which the peculiar value of cocoa depends is the theobromine, an alkaloid substance, which till recently was supposed to be distinct from, though closely allied to, the theine of tea and coffee. It is now, however, known that the alkaloid in these, and in two or three other substances similarly used, is identical, and their physiological value is consequently the same. The fat, or cocoa-butter, is a firm, solid white substance, at ordinary temperature, having an agreeable taste and odor, and very remarkable for its freedom from any tendency to become rancid. It consists essentially of stearin, with a little olein, and is used in surgical practice, and in France as a material for soap and pomade manufacture.

" The starch grains present in raw cocoa are small in size, and of a character so peculiar that there is no difficulty in distinguishing them under the microscope from any other starch granules. As an article of food cocoa differs essentially from both tea and coffee. While only an infusion of these substances is used, leaving a large proportion of their total weight unconsumed, the entire substance of the cocoa-seeds is prepared as an emulsion for drinking, and the whole is thus utilized within the system. While the contents of a cup of tea or coffee can thus only be regarded as stimulant in its effect, and almost entirely destitute of essential nutritive properties, a cup of prepared cocoa is really a most nourishing article of diet, as, in addition to the value of the theobromine it contains, it introduces into the system no inconsiderable portion of valuable nitrogenous and oleaginous elements."

M. Arthur Mangin, in his valuable work, "*Le Cacao et le Chocolat,*" published in 1862, gives some very good reasons for promoting the use of cocoa. He says : —

" Cocoa cannot be considered in any respect an article of luxury. It is not a *dainty;* its hygienic and nutritive properties are unquestionable and unquestioned, and its being endowed with an aroma and flavor which please the sense of smell and the palate is no reason at all for its not being reckoned among articles of food, properly so called. Its cultivation, transport and preparation furnish occupation and support to a multitude of laborers, and its consumption should be respected and encouraged by all wise governments, not only because it is physically beneficial, but, and we do not hesitate to say it, because it is *morally* salutary.

" Coffee, of which much good can honestly be said, is, however, open to much criticism, as well on account of its physiological effects as its influence on public morals. It can be abused and misused.

Its infusion is an exciting beverage, which does not agree with every one, and which may, when used to excess, cause serious consequences, decidedly affect the health, and even disturb the intellectual faculties. Coffee, moreover, easily becomes a pretext for debauch. It is consumed in the most respectable houses; but also in *cafés*, liquor saloons and disreputable places, with the accompaniments of alcoholic liquors, tobacco-smoke, coarse words, and unlawful games.

" It is impossible to impute the like effects to chocolate. Its use can never degenerate into abuse, and it can never, like coffee, become a poison, even a slow poison. And then, whatever certain casuists may say, chocolate is decidedly a food, not a beverage. More, it is, above all, the food of sober, orderly, and peaceable folk. It is found only on the family table, at parties of good society, or in public establishments frequented either by well-bred people or hard-working mechanics. We do not play cards or smoke while we drink chocolate, and after it we take no brandy; we drink, perhaps, a glass of cold water, and go peaceably back to our work or to look after our affairs.

" The well-known proverb, ' People are known by the company they keep,' would lose none of its force if altered to read: ' Tell me what you eat and drink, and I will tell you who you are.' Breakfast, especially, is the characteristic repast, which gives the surest indications as to the morality of civilized men. The man who eats a substantial meat breakfast, and follows it up with coffee and liquors, may certainly be a very honest man, but he is not a temperate man, and one might wager that after such a repast he will do very little. Be assured, on the contrary, that he who breakfasts on milk, coffee, or chocolate has few physical wants; that his sensuality, if he be sensual, is mild and

moderate, and that the man in him has the
mastery over he animal.   Let governments load with high duties all spirituous
liquors, — luxurious beverages for the rich,
but utter poison for the people, — agents of
depravity, demoralization, and degenera-
tion, equally fatal to public morals and
public health; let them impose an arbi-
trary tax on tobacco, and even monopolize
the sale at fictitious prices; let them do
likewise with playing-cards and other
articles which supply merely imaginary
wants, — these are measures whose political
legitimacy or economic utility may be at-
tacked, but which cannot be contested as
contrary to the popular interest, or to the
increase of its comfort or its moral im-
provement.

" Cocoa is, on the contrary, among the
few articles — it is perhaps the only one
—whose sale should be not only released
from all constraint, but encouraged and
extended, because it is the only article of

food to which may be applied the apparently strange and paradoxical qualification — *morally improving food.* We have just shown that this qualification suits it in all respects. It is proved, beside, that cocoa enters too largely into popular consumption, that it forms too great an addition to the sum of the food substances already existing, for it to be reckoned henceforth among luxuries subject to sumptuary laws."

Dr. Edmund A. Parkes, F.R.S., in his " Manual of Practical Hygiene, prepared especially for use in the Medical Service of the Army" (London, 1864), says : —

" Although the theobromine of cocoa is now known to be identical with theine and caffeine, the composition of cocoa removes it widely from tea and coffee. The quantity of fat varies even in the same sort of cocoa. The ash contains a large quantity of phosphate of potash. The larger quantity

of fat makes it a very nourishing article of
diet, and it is therefore useful in weak
states of the system, and for healthy men
under circumstances of great exertion. It
has even been compared to milk. In
South America cocoa and maize cakes are
used by travellers, and the large amount
of agreeable nourishment in small bulk
enables several days' supplies to be easily
carried. By roasting, the starch is changed
into dextrin, the amount of margaric acid
increases, and an empyrematic aromatic
substance is formed."

Baron von Liebig, the famous chemist,
says : —

" It is a perfect food, as wholesome as
delicious, a beneficent restorer of exhausted
power ; but its quality must be good, and
it must be carefully prepared. It is highly
nourishing and easily digested, and is fitted
to repair wasted strength, preserve health,
and prolong life. It agrees with dry tem-

peraments and convalescents ; with mothers who nurse their children ; with those whose occupations oblige them to undergo severe mental strains; with public speakers, and with all those who give to work a portion of the time needed for sleep. It soothes both stomach and brain, and for this reason, as well as for others, it is the best friend of those engaged in literary pursuits."

François Joseph Victor Broussais, a celebrated physician and member of the French Institute, says : —

" Chocolate of good quality, well made, properly cooked, is one of the best aliments that I have yet found for my patients and for myself. This delicious food calms the fever, nourishes adequately the patient, and tends to restore him to health. I would even add that I attribute many cures of chronic dyspepsia to the regular use of chocolate."

Christoph Wilhelm Hufeland, the distinguished German physician, says : —

" I recommend good chocolate to nervous, excitable persons ; also to the weak, debilitated, and infirm ; to children and women. I have obtained excellent results from it in many cases of chronic diseases of the digestive organs."

Dr. Karl Ernest Bock, of Leipsic, author of a " *Traité de Pathologie et de Diagnostic*," says : —

" The nervousness and peevishness of our times are chiefly attributable to tea and coffee ; the digestive organs of confirmed coffee-drinkers are in a state of chronic derangement, which reacts upon the brain, producing fretful and lachrymose moods. Cocoa and chocolate are neutral in their physical effects, and are really the most harmless of our fashionable drinks."

Jean Baptiste Alphonse Chevalier, in his treatise on chocolate, says : —

" Cocoa and chocolate are a complete food ; coffee and tea are not food. Cocoa gives one-third its weight in starch and one-half in cocoa-butter ; and, converted into chocolate by the addition of sugar, it realizes the idea of a complete aliment, wholesome and eminently hygienic. The shells of the bean contain the same principles as the kernels, and the extract, obtained by an infusion of the shells in sweetened milk, forms a mixture at once agreeable to the taste, and an advantageous substitute for tea and coffee."

Mme. de Sevigné, in one of her letters to her daughter, says : —

" I took chocolate night before last to digest my dinner, in order to have a good supper. I took some yesterday for nourishment, so as to be able to fast until night. What I consider amusing about chocolate is that it acts according to the wishes of the one who takes it."

It will be observed that Brillat-Savarin corroborates this statement as to the value of chocolate as an aid to digestion.

" The cocoa-nut," says M. Payen, in " *Des Substances Alimentaires*," " has in its composition more azote than wheat flour, about twenty times as much fatty matter, a considerable proportion of starch, and an agreeable aroma which excites the appetite. We are entirely disposed to admit that this substance contains a remarkable nutritive power. Besides, direct experience has proved this to be the case. In fact, cocoa, closely combined with an equal or two-thirds weight of sugar, forming the article well-known under the name of chocolate, constitutes a food, substantial in all respects, and capable of sustaining the strength in travelling."

And, a little farther on, he adds : —

" Cocoa and chocolate, in consequence of their elementary composition, and of the direct or indirect addition of sugar before their consumption, constitute a food, respiratory, or capable of maintaining animal heat, by means of the starch, sugar, gum, and fatty matter which they contain ; they are also articles of food favorable to the maintenance or development of the adipose secretions, by reason of the fatty matter (cocoa-butter) belonging to them ; and, finally, they assist in the maintenance and increase of the tissues by means of their congeneric azote substances, which assimilate therewith."

Etienne François Geoffroy, the distinguished French physician and professor of medicine and pharmacy in the College of France, says, in his " *Traité de Matiére Médicale*" : —

" The drinking of chocolate, especially of that made with milk, is recommended

to persons affected with phthisis or consumption; and, in fact, it supplies a juice
which is nourishing, substantial, and
smooth, which *deadens the acrimony of the
humors;* provided, as we have said, that the
cocoa is properly roasted, and mixed with
a very small quantity of spices."

The French officer, from whose work on
the "Natural History of Chocolate" we have
already quoted, after describing the different methods of raising and curing the fruit
and preparing it for food (which it is not
worth while to reproduce here, as the
methods have essentially changed during
the last fifty years), goes on to demonstrate,
as the result of actual experiment, that
chocolate is a substance " very temperate,
very nourishing, and of easy digestion;
very proper to repair the exhausted spirits
and decayed strength; and very suitable to
preserve the health and prolong the lives
of old men."

" I could produce several instances," he says, " in favor of this excellent nourishment ; but I shall content myself with two only, equally certain and decisive, in proof of its goodness. The first is an experiment of chocolate's being taken for the only nourishment, — made by a surgeon's wife of Martinico : she had lost, by a very deplorable accident, her lower jaw, which reduced her to such a condition that she did not know how to subsist. She was not capable of taking anything solid, and not rich enough to live upon jellies and nourishing broths. In this strait she determined to take three dishes of chocolate, prepared after the manner of the country, one in the morning, one at noon, and one at night. There chocolate is nothing else but cocoa kernels dissolved in hot water, with sugar, and seasoned with a bit of cinnamon. This new way of life succeeded so well that she has lived a long while since, more lively and robust than before this accident.

"I had the second relation from a gentleman of Martinico, and one of my friends not capable of a falsity.

"He assured me that in his neighborhood an infant of four months old unfortunately lost his nurse, and its parents, not being able to put it to another, resolved, through necessity to feed it with chocolate. The success was very happy, for the infant came on to a miracle, and was neither less healthy nor less vigorous than those who are brought up by the best nurses.

"Before chocolate was known in Europe good old wine was called the milk of old men; but this title is now applied with greater reason to chocolate; since its use has become so common that it has been perceived that chocolate is, with respect to them, what milk is to infants. In reality, if one examines the nature of chocolate a little, with respect to the constitution of aged persons, it seems as though the one was made on purpose to remedy the defects of the other, and that it is truly the panacea of old age.

" Our life, as a famous physician observes, is, as it were, a continual growing dry; but yet this kind of natural consumption is imperceptible to an advanced age, when the radical moisture is consumed more sensibly. The more balmy and volatile parts of the blood are dissipated by little and little; the salts, disengaging from the sulphurs, manifest themselves; the acid appears, which is the fruitful source of chronic diseases. The ligaments, the tendons, and the cartilages have scarce any of the unctuosity left, which rendered them so supple and so pliant in youth. The skin grows wrinkled as well within as without; in a word, all the solid parts grow dry or bony.

" One may say that nature has formed chocolate with every virtue proper to remedy these inconveniences.

" The volatile sulphur with which it

abounds is proper to supply the place of
that which the blood loses every day
through age; it blunts and sheathes the
points of the salts, and restores the usual
softness to the blood, like as spirit of wine,
united with spirit of salt, makes a soft
liquor of a violent corrosive. The same
sulphurous unctuosity at the same time
spreads itself in the solid parts, and gives
them, in some sense, their natural suppleness. It bestows on the membranes, the
tendons, the ligaments and the cartilages, a
kind of oil which renders them smooth and
flexible. Thus the equilibrium between
the fluids and solids is, in some measure,
reëstablished; the wheels and springs
of our machine mended; health is preserved and life prolonged. These are not
the consequences of philosophical reflec-
tions, but of a thousand experiments which
mutually confirm each other; among a
great number of which the following alone
shall suffice : —

" There lately died at Martinico a counsellor, about a hundred years old, who, for thirty years past, lived on nothing but chocolate and biscuit. He sometimes, indeed, had a little soup at dinner, but never any fish, flesh, or other victuals. He was, nevertheless, so vigorous and nimble that at fourscore and five he could get on horseback without stirrups.

" Chocolate is not only proper to prolong the life of aged people, but also of those whose constitution is lean and dry, or weak and cacochymical, or who use violent exercises, or whose employments oblige them to an intense application of mind, which makes them very faintish. To all these it agrees perfectly well, and becomes to them an altering diet."

VI.

COCOA—BUTTER.

" AS the oil (or butter) of cocoa is very
anodyne, or an easer of pain, it is
excellent, taken inwardly, to cure hoarse-
ness and to blunt the sharpness of the salts
that irritate the lungs.   In using it must be
melted and mixed with a sufficient quantity
of sugar candy and made into lozenges,
which must be held in the mouth until
the substance melts quite away, so that it
can be swallowed gently.   Taken season-
ably the oil is also a wonderful antidote
against corrosive poisons.

"It is the best and most natural pomatum
for ladies to clear and plump the skin
when it is dry, rough, or shrivelled, without making it appear either fat or shining.
The Spanish women at Mexico use it

very much, and it is highly esteemed by them.

" The leaving off the practice of anointing the body with oil can be attributed to nothing else but the ill smell and other disagreeable effects that attended it ; but if oil of chocolate was used instead of oil of olives those inconveniences would be avoided, because it has no smell and dries entirely into the skin. Nothing certainly would be more advantageous, especially for aged persons, than to renew this custom, which has been authorized by the experience of antiquity.

" Apothecaries ought to make use of this, preferably to all others, as the basis of their balsams, because all other oils grow rancid, and this does not.

" There is nothing so proper as this to keep arms from rusting, because it contains less water than any other oil made use of for that purpose.

" In the West Indies they make use of

this oil to cure the piles. Others use it to ease gout pains, applying it hot to the part, with a compress dipped in it, which they cover with a hot napkin. It may be used after the same manner for the rheumatism."

M. Arthur Mangin says : —

"When pure and freshly extracted cocoa-butter is of a pale yellow color; its consistency is about that of tallow. Its odor is faint, but sweet, and its taste pleasant. When thoroughly purified, and protected from heat, air, and dampness, it may be preserved, without perceptible alteration, for several years.

"It is insoluble in water, hardly soluble in alcohol, completely soluble in sulphuric ether and the essential oil of turpentine. Its density is 0.91. It softens perceptibly at 24° or 25° (*Centigrade; i.e.*, 56 or 57 *Fahrenheit*), but melts only at 29°, and becomes entirely liquid only at 35° to 40°. It cannot boil without being decomposed.

It contains, according to M. Boussingault, carbon, .766 ; hydrogen, .119 ; oxygen, .115. Cocoa-butter formerly played a tolerably important part in medicine, by reason of the numerous properties attributed to it. It was called a pectoral, an expectorant, a humective, a demulcent, an emollient, a refrigerative, etc., etc. It was prescribed for persons suffering from or suspected of chest diseases, nervous coughs, bronchitis, etc., and it was combined with kermes, ipecacuanha, etc., to make pills, emulsions, opiates, and other remedies.

" At present it is no longer prescribed for internal use ; but pharmacists, as well as perfumers, make it the basis of many pomades and ointments, whose use is, we are assured, most beneficial, and, at all events, most agreeable. Cocoa-butter, pure or simply combined with an oil which renders it more or less unctuous, is one of the smoothest, most fragrant, and, if we may be allowed the expression, most *savory*, pomades which can be used for the hair or skin, and it is astonishing that there should be preferred to it so many equivocal compounds whose exorbitant price is justified by not one of the properties claimed for them by the puffs of perfumers."

"This concentrated oil," says M. Delcher, " is the best and most natural of all the pomades which ladies, who possess a too dry skin can use to make it smooth, soft, and polished, without any greasy or shining appearance, which is produced by most of the pomades advertised for the purpose.

"I agree," continues the same author, " with the opinion of M. Plisson, who advises the use of cocoa-butter pomade for women who suffer from acrid eruptions, cracked lips, breast, etc. The Spaniards of Mexico understand the value of these preparations; but, as in France, this concentrated oil hardens too much, it is necessary to mix it with the oil of the ben-nut,

or of sweet almonds. If the ancient custom of the Greeks and Romans should be
revived, of anointing one's self with oil to
give suppleness to the limbs and to guard
against rheumatism, the oil of cocoa should
be chosen for the purpose.

" Considered as food, and as a medicinal
substance, cocoa-butter possesses the same
fundamental property as other fat. It supplies to respiration the necessary combus-
tible elements, and renders it, in consequence, more easy and active. It may,
therefore, be administered with advantage
to persons suffering from affections of the
chest, and possesses the advantage, in common with only a very small number of
substances of the same kind, that the most
fastidious and obstinate patient may take it
for the whole of his life without disgust."

RECEIPTS.

RECEIPTS.

VII.

DIFFERENT METHODS OF PREPARING DRINKS.

THERE are many different methods of preparing cocoa and chocolate for drinking. The Mexicans are in the habit of preparing it with *atole*, a kind of pap made of maize, which is their most ancient and common beverage, and which they mix hot, in equal quantities with the chocolate dissolved in hot water, and drink directly.[1] They also dissolve the chocolate

---

[1] " I remember," says Prof. Eaton, " some that was brought home from Mexico by the officers of Gen. Zachary Taylor's army. The cakes were of half a pound weight, or so, and were made of very coarsely pounded cocoa.

in cold water, stirring it with the chocolate
stick, and skim off the froth into another
vessel, then put the remaining chocolate
over the fire with sugar enough to sweeten
it, and as soon as it boils pour it over the
froth, and drink it.

The inhabitants of St. Domingo put
chocolate into a vessel with a little water,
and boil it till it is dissolved; then add the
necessary water and sugar, let it boil again
till an unctuous froth is formed, and drink
it in this state.

The Indians of New Spain make use of

They were well sweetened, and contained a large proportion
of some starchy material. For a drink the chocolate is
broken into small pieces and placed with water in a red
earthen pot, an upright cylindrical pot, and heated.   When
the chocolate is boiled enough it is stirred violently with a
sort of dasher, much like that of an old-fashioned churn,
except that the handle is rolled between the hands rather
than worked up and down. The chocolate is beaten into a
foam, which the old travellers declared remained so stiff
after the chocolate was cold that it could be cut up and
eaten in mouthfuls. This effect must have been due to the
quantity of starch, or, most likely, fine maize-meal, in the
drink, rather than to any special skill in milling it."

cold chocolate in their festivals, prepared
by milling pure chocolate in cold water,
skimming off the froth into another vessel,
then adding sugar to the remaining liquid,
and pouring it from a great height on
the froth. This chocolate is exceedingly
cold.

Iced chocolate is used in many parts of
Italy, where it is the custom to cool almost
all beverages upon snow or ice.

The Spanish method of making chocolate is to mix it so thick that a spoon can
stand upright in the mixture; then to
drink iced water after it by way of dilut-
ing it.

Chocolate is usually milled in a tin vessel,
within which a wheel, somewhat smaller
in circumference than the vessel, is fixed
to a stem which passes through the lid,
and, being turned rapidly between the
palms of the hands, bruises and mixes the
chocolate with the water. Chocolate should
be first milled off the fire, then put on and

left to simmer for some time, after which
it is milled again till perfectly smooth, and
free from sediment. Any ladle or stick
which effectually mixes the chocolate with
the water may be substituted for the milling stick. Chocolate in powder does not
require milling. Chocolate should never
be made until wanted, as it is spoiled by
reheating. Chocolate may be made in an
iron pot or stewpan, a chocolate-pot, or
Chocolatière. — *The Dessert Book.*

Plain Chocolate (1).

The quantity of chocolate for a certain
quantity of milk is according to taste. Two
ounces of chocolate make a good cup of it,
and rather thick. Break the chocolate in
pieces, put it in a tin saucepan with a teaspoonful of water to an ounce of chocolate,
and set it on a rather slow fire. Stir now
and then till thoroughly melted. While
the chocolate is melting set the quantity
of milk desired in another tin saucepan on

the fire, and as soon as it rises, and when
the chocolate is melted as directed above,
turn the milk into the chocolate little by
little, beating well at the same time with an
egg-beater. Keep beating and boiling after
being mixed, for three or four minutes ; take
off and serve. If both chocolate and milk
are good it will be frothy, and no better or
more nutritious drink can be had. — *Pierre
Blot*.

Plain Chocolate (2).

Scrape one ounce (one of the small
squares) of Baker's or any plain chocolate,
fine ; add to this two tablespoonfuls of
sugar, and put into a small saucepan with
one tablespoonful of hot water ; stir over a
hot fire for a minute or two, until it is perfectly smooth and glossy ; then stir it all
into a quart of boiling milk, or half milk
and half water ; mix thoroughly and serve
immediately. If the chocolate is desired
richer take twice as much chocolate, sugar,
and water. Made in this way chocolate

is perfectly smooth and free from oily particles. If it is allowed to boil after the chocolate is added to the milk it becomes oily and loses its fine flavor. —*Maria Parloa.*

Frothed Chocolate.

One cup of boiling water; three pints of fresh milk; three tablespoonfuls of Baker's chocolate, grated; five eggs, the whites only beaten light; two tablespoonfuls of sugar, powdered for froth. Sweeten the chocolate to taste; heat the milk to scalding; wet up the chocolate with the boiling water, and when the milk is hot stir this into it; simmer gently ten minutes, stirring frequently; boil up briskly once; take from the fire, sweeten to taste, taking care not to make it too sweet, and stir in the whites of two eggs, whipped stiff, without sugar; pour into the chocolate-pot or pitcher, which should be well heated. Have ready in a cream-pitcher the remaining whites, whipped up with the powdered sugar; cover the surface of each cup with sweetened *méringue* before distributing to the guests.

Chocolate or cocoa is a favorite luncheon beverage, and many ladies, especially those who have spent much time abroad, have adopted the French habit of breakfasting upon rolls and a cup of chocolate. — *Marion Harland.*

Milled Chocolate.

Three heaping tablespoonfuls of grated chocolate; one quart of milk; wet the chocolate with boiling water, scald the milk, and stir in the chocolate-paste; simmer ten minutes; then, if you have no regular " muller," put your syllabub-churn into the boiling liquid and churn steadily, without taking from the fire, until it is a yeasty froth; pour into a chocolate-pitcher and serve at once.

This is esteemed a great delicacy by chocolate-lovers, and is easily made. — *Marion Harland.*

Baker's Premium No. 1 Chocolate.

Scrape fine about one square of a cake,
which is one ounce; add to it about an
equal weight of sugar; put these into a
pint of perfectly *boiling* milk and water,
of each one-half, and immediately mill or
stir them well for two or three minutes,
until the sugar and chocolate are well dissolved. Some think ten or twelve minutes'
boiling improves it.

Baker's Vanilla Chocolate.

This may be prepared with either milk
or water, according to the taste of the consumer. For one cup of chocolate scrape
fine one of the oblong divisions and fully
dissolve it in a very little *boiling* water.
Put one cup of milk or water in a saucepan, and when it is at the highest boiling-
point add the chocolate. Then allow it
to simmer from five to seven minutes, but
not to boil.

Baker's Breakfast Cocoa.

Into a breakfast-cup put a teaspoonful of the powder, add a tablespoonful of boiling water and mix thoroughly ; then add equal parts of boiling water and boiled milk, and sugar to the taste. Boiling two or three minutes will improve it.

Baker's Cocoa-Paste.

Put two teaspoonfuls of paste into a tea-cup ; pour upon it a little boiling water, and stir it until it is dissolved ; then fill the cup with boiling water, and stir again ; add cream or milk, if agreeable. Two or three minutes' boiling improves it.

Baker's Eagle French Chocolate.

Into a pint of boiling milk and water (of each one-half, or other proportions if more agreeable) throw two oblong divisions of the chocolate cake, previously cut fine ; then boil it from five to seven minutes longer, stirring it frequently.

German Sweet Chocolate.

Into one pint of boiling milk and water (of each one-half) throw two squares of chocolate scraped fine ; then boil it five minutes longer or more, stirring frequently.

Baker's Racahout des Arabes.

Dissolve two tablespoonfuls of Racahout in a little cold milk. Heat gradually a quart of milk to boiling ; add the above and let it boil (stirring meanwhile) until it begins to thicken. To enrich for dessert, add two eggs to the mixture before putting it into the boiling milk. Strain the whole when cooked.

Baker's Broma.

Dissolve a large tablespoonful of broma in as much warm water ; then pour upon it a pint of boiling milk and water, in equal proportions, and boil it two minutes longer, stirring it frequently ; add sugar at pleasure.

Baker's Cocoa Shells.

Take a small quantity of cocoa shells (say two ounces), pour upon them three pints of boiling water ; boil rapidly thirty or forty minutes ; allow it to settle or strain, and add cream or boiled milk and sugar at pleasure.

Baker's Prepared Cocoa.

To one pint of milk and one pint of cold water add three tablespoonfuls of cocoa ; boil fifteen or twenty minutes. Any other proportions of milk and water make a pleasant beverage.

Baker's Premium Cracked Cocoa.

Use the same quantity as of coffee. Cocoa in this form needs thorough and continued boiling to extract its full strength. By adding a small quantity of cocoa daily the consumer will have a highly flavored cup of cocoa at a trifling expense.

French Chocolat au lait (Chocolate with milk).

Place the chocolate, cut into small pieces, in a saucepan over a *slow* fire, in order that the chocolate may dissolve gradually and not adhere to the pan. When the chocolate is completely melted pour boiling milk upon it in small quantities, and stir rapidly. After adding the requisite quantity of milk let the mixture come to the boiling-point for an instant, and you will have a light and most agreeable chocolate.

Chocolat à l'eau (Chocolate with water).

Follow the directions given above, using water instead of milk. When the full allowance of water has been added to the chocolate the mixture should boil for ten minutes, and be stirred continually.

Spanish Chocolate.

For one cup of chocolate scrape fine *two* oblong divisions, and fully dissolve it

in a very little boiling water. Put one
cup of milk or water in a saucepan, and
when it is at the highest boiling-point add
the chocolate. Allow it to simmer for
five or ten minutes, but not to boil, stirring
all the time.

The Spanish method of making chocolate is to mix it so thick that a spoon can
stand upright in the mixture.

Egg Chocolate.

Dissolve the chocolate in boiling water;
beat the yolk of an egg to foam in a bowl,
and pour the chocolate slowly over it, stirring constantly all the time.

Chocolate, one cake; water, one cup;
yolk of one egg.

German Egg Chocolate.

Put four ounces of fine chocolate, dissolved in a little hot water, into a perfectly
clean stewpan with three large cups of
water and one ounce of powdered sugar,

and set it over the fire. Beat the yolks of
two eggs to foam in a cup of water, and
stir them, with fifteen drops of rose-water
and the same quantity of orange-flower-
water, into the chocolate as soon as it
begins to simmer. Let it stand a few
moments longer over the fire without boiling, stirring it all the time; then take it
off and serve it with biscuit or *marchpau.*

Chocolate, four ounces; water, three
cups; sugar, one ounce; yolks of five
eggs; rose-water, fifteen drops; orange-
water, fifteen drops. Boil up once.

Parisian Egg Chocolate.

For three cups of chocolate dissolve
three ounces of the best chocolate in four
cups of water, and set it over the fire; beat
the yolks of two eggs to foam, and stir
them into the chocolate as soon as it begins
to froth; skim off the froth into warm
chocolate-cups until they are heaped full,
then hold a shovelful of burning coals to

each till the froth is converted to a light crust, when serve.

The chocolate froths better when finely powdered sugar is mixed with the yolks of eggs, and still better when froth-cakes are added, prepared in the following manner : —

Beat the whites of a dozen eggs to froth, and stir in powdered sugar till the mass is of the consistency of a stiff paste. Mould the paste on a large plate into small cakes, about the size and shape of an ordinary-sized hazel-nut, and dry them in the sun or in a warm room.

As soon as the egg-yolks have been stirred into the chocolate add as many of these cakes as there are cups of the liquid, and continue to stir it until the whole mass becomes froth. Care must be taken to keep the chocolate near the boiling-point, whether on or off the fire, without letting it boil over.

Chocolate, three ounces; water, four

cups; yolks of eggs, two. Boil, and mill
to froth.

Wine Chocolate.

Set half a bottle of good white wine,
three ounces of chocolate, and one ounce
of powdered sugar over the fire; beat the
yolks of four eggs to foam, with a little
wine, and add it to the chocolate as soon
as it begins to simmer; stir it for a few
minutes, then take it from the fire and
serve. This is an excellent winter beverage. — *Dessert Book.*

Chocolate Wine.

Infuse in a bottle of Madeira, Marsala or
raisin wine four ounces of chocolate, and
sugar if required. In three or four days
strain and bottle. — *Confectioner's Journal.*

PUDDINGS.

Chocolate Pudding (1).

Half a cake of chocolate grated (Baker's,
two cakes in one package); vanilla to

flavor; small half pint of soda-cracker crumbs; butter size of an egg; one-half pint of boiled milk; whites of six eggs; one-half cup of sugar; salt; boil in a mould for one hour. To be eaten hot.

SAUCE.

Yolks of six eggs; one tumbler of sherry wine; one-half large cup of sugar; beat the yolks very light; put the sugar in the sherry, then heat the wine; when it is very hot add the beaten yolks; stir quickly one way until it thickens to a very rich cream. To be eaten cold. — *Choice Receipts.*

Chocolate Pudding (2).

For six persons use one quart of milk, one pint of stale bread, four eggs, one ounce of grated chocolate, half a cupful of granulated sugar, three tablespoonfuls of powdered sugar, half a teaspoonful of vanilla extract, and one teaspoonful of salt.

Soak the bread and milk together for

two hours; then mash the bread fine by
pressing it with a spoon against the side
of the bowl. Put the chocolate, three
tablespoonfuls of the granulated sugar and
one tablespoonful of boiling water in a
small stewpan, and stir over a hot fire
until the liquid becomes smooth and glossy;
now take from the fire and add a few
spoonfuls of bread and milk. Stir until
the mixture is thin and smooth; then add
it to the bread and milk.

Beat the yolks and one white of the egg
with the remainder of the granulated sugar;
add this mixture and the salt to the bread
and milk; pour into a pudding-dish and
bake in a slow oven for forty minutes.

Now beat the three remaining whites to
a stiff, dry froth, and, with a spoon, beat
into them three tablespoonfuls of powdered sugar and the vanilla. Spread this
méringue over the pudding and cook for a
quarter of an hour longer with the oven
door open. Serve with whipped cream.

When it is inconvenient to use cream the *méringue* will suffice as a sauce. If a strong flavor of chocolate be liked use two ounces instead of one. — *Maria Parloa.*

Chocolate Pudding (3).

One pint of rich milk; two tablespoonfuls of corn-starch; one scant half cup of sugar; whites of four eggs; a little salt; flavoring; beat the eggs to a stiff froth; dissolve the corn-starch in a little of the milk; stir the sugar into the remainder of the milk, which place on the fire; when it begins to boil add the dissolved corn-starch; stir constantly for a few minutes, when it will become a smooth paste; now stir in the beaten whites of the eggs, and let it remain a little longer to cook the eggs; flavor the whole with vanilla; now take out a third of the pudding, flavor the remainder in the kettle with a bar of chocolate, softened, mashed, and dissolved with a little milk; put half the chocolate pudding in the bottom of a mould (which has been wet with water); smooth the top; next make a layer with the white pudding (the third taken out); smooth it also; next the remainder of the chocolate pudding.

Serve with whipped cream, or a boiled custard, made with the yolks of the eggs and flavored with vanilla. — *Mrs. Mary F. Henderson.*

Chocolate Pudding (4).

One quart milk; three ounces grated vanilla chocolate; three tablespoonfuls of corn starch; two eggs; half a cup pulverized sugar: boil the milk; stir in the chocolate, starch, sugar, and beaten yolks of the eggs; bake; when the pudding is cold beat the whites of the two eggs to a froth; stir in half a cup of pulverized sugar; place this frosting on the pudding and serve. — *Choice Receipts.*

Chocolate Mixture.

Five tablespoonfuls of grated chocolate with enough cream or milk to wet it, one cupful of sugar, and one egg well beaten. Stir the ingredients over the fire until thoroughly mixed; then flavor with vanilla. — *Mrs. Mary F. Henderson.*

CAKE, ETC.

Chocolate Cake (1).

Two cups of sugar; four tablespoonfuls of butter rubbed in with the sugar; four eggs, whites and yolks beaten separately; one cup of sweet milk; three heaping cups of flour; one teaspoonful of cream tartar, sifted into flour; one-half teaspoonful of soda melted in hot water; bake in jelly-cake tins.

FILLING.

Whites of two eggs, beaten to a froth; one cup of powdered sugar; one-quarter pound of grated chocolate, wet in one tablespoonful of cream; one teaspoonful vanilla; beat the sugar into the whipped whites, then the chocolate; whisk all together hard for three minutes before adding the vanilla; let the cake get quite cold before you spread it; reserve a little of the mixture for the top, and beat more sugar into this to form a firm icing. — *Marion Harland.*

Chocolate Cake (2).

Beat one and a quarter pounds of sugar and ten ounces of butter to a cream; whisk the whites and the yolks of ten eggs separately, after which mix and beat them together, and add them gradually to the sugar and butter; now add and stir in six ounces of cocoa-paste or chocolate grated and melted in just sufficient boiling water to form a thickish paste; next add and stir in one pint of milk, then add one and three-quarter pounds of flour that has been thoroughly sifted together with one and a half ounces of Royal baking powder; beat all lightly and quickly to a smooth mass and bake in buttered cake-pans in a quick oven; or it may be baked in layers in jelly-cake pans, and filled with the following cream: Take six ounces of sugar, two whole eggs, and the yolks of three more, two or three tablespoonfuls of grated chocolate, one tablespoonful of corn-starch and one pint of milk; beat the sugar, the two eggs, and the grated chocolate to a cream; beat the three yolks and the corn-starch together, and then add them to the chocolate mixture and work all together till smooth, then stir in the milk and cook to a custard; when cold spread a layer of it over a sheet of the cake, on top of which lay another sheet of the cake, which spread in like manner with custard, on top of which place a third sheet of the cake, over which sift finely powdered sugar. — *Confectioner's Journal.*

Chocolate Cake (3).

One very full cup of butter ; two cups of sugar ; three and a half cups of flour ; one cup, not quite full, of milk ; five eggs ; one teaspoonful cream of tartar ; half teaspoonful soda. — *Icing:* Whites of two eggs ; one and a half cups of pulverized sugar ; two teaspoonfuls of essence of vanilla ; six tablespoonfuls of grated vanilla (Baker's) chocolate ; beat the yolks of the five and the whites of the three eggs separately, until they are as light as they can be made ; put the cream of tartar in the flour ; dissolve the soda in a little of the milk ; rub the butter and sugar to a cream ; add the eggs, milk, flour, and soda ; pour the mixture into a large, shallow pan, well buttered, and put it in the oven. While it is baking make the icing by beating the whites of the two eggs to a stiff froth, and stir the sugar in well ; add the grated chocolate and the essence of vanilla ; when

the cake is done turn it out on a sieve;
while hot put on the icing. — *Choice Receipts.*

Chocolate Cake (4).

One cup of butter; two cups of sugar;
three cups of flour; half cup sweet milk;
half teaspoonful soda; one teaspoonful of
cream tartar; seven eggs. — *Chocolate
Cream:* Quarter of a pound of Baker's
best vanilla chocolate; one gill of sweet
milk; one egg; sugar to taste. Rub butter
and sugar together; beat the seven eggs
until they are very light; put the cream of
tartar in the flour and the soda in the milk;
mix all well, and bake in four Washington-
pie plates. While this is baking scald the
gill of milk and the chocolate together;
beat one egg thoroughly and stir it in; add
sugar to taste. When the cake is done
spread the chocolate cream between the
layers and upon the tops of the cakes. —
Choice Receipts.

Chocolate Cake (5).

One cupful of butter; two cupfuls of
sugar; three cupfuls of flour; one cupful
of milk; four eggs well beaten; one teaspoonful of soda; two teaspoonfuls of cream
of tartar.   Bake in Washington-pie plates.
Put a layer of the chocolate mixture between
and on the top and sides of the cake.

Chocolate Cake (6).

One cup of butter, two of sugar, three of
flour, four eggs, and a cup three-quarters
full of grated chocolate.   Stir the butter
and sugar to a cream ; add the beaten yolks
of the eggs, beat well, then the whites
beaten to a stiff froth alternately with the
flour ; beat very hard ; stir in the chocolate
and bake in one large cake or in square tin
pans. — *Sara T. Paul.*

Chocolate Cakes (1).

The whites of eight eggs ; half a cake of
chocolate, grated ; one pound of sugar ; six

ounces of flour; beat the eggs to a stiff froth, add the sugar, then stir in the chocolate and flour. Butter flat tins, and drop on the mixture, not too closely, as the cakes will spread. Bake a few minutes in a quick oven. — *Sara T. Paul.*

Chocolate Cakes (2).

Put the yolks of three eggs in a bowl, with four ounces of powdered sugar; beat them well until slightly consistent, and add to them an ounce and a half of flour, an ounce of corn-starch, a few drops of extract of vanilla, and mix all well together. Beat up the whites of your eggs very stiff, and stir them lightly with your other ingredients. Put it in a cornucopia made of stiff paper, with a hole in the end, through which press it on a pan (on which you have spread a sheet of white paper), and form it into small rounds about the size of a fifty-cent piece. Send them to a gentle oven until they are quite firm; then let them become cold, and cut them all the same size with a small, round cutter. Spread a layer of peach or other marmalade on the half of your cakes, which cover with the other half. Melt about two ounces of chocolate in about two tablespoonfuls of water. Put in a saucepan on the fire half a pound of sugar, with half a glass of water; boil for about eight to ten minutes; lift out some of the sugar with a spoon, drop it into cold water; place it between the thumb and third finger, and, if you may draw the sugar out into a long fine thread, without breaking, you have reached the desired result; then put your chocolate in a bowl, add your sugar, stirring until beginning to thicken. Take as many little wooden skewers as you have cakes, sharpen them to a fine point, stick one into each cake, which dip into your chocolate and sugar, covering it entirely. Put a colander upside-down on a table, and in the holes place the ends of your sticks, thereby allowing the cakes on the opposite end to dry; after which remove your cakes from the sticks, and serve when needed. — *Pierre Caron.*

Chocolate Macaroons.

Melt on a slow fire and in a tin pan three ounces of chocolate without sugar (known as Baker's chocolate); then work it to a thick paste with one pound of pulverized sugar and three whites of eggs. Roll the mixture down to the thickness of about one-quarter of an inch; cut it in small round pieces with a paste-cutter, either plain or scalloped; butter a pan slightly and dust it with flour and sugar, half of each; place the pieces of paste or mixture in and bake in a hot, but not quick oven. Serve cold. — *Pierre Blot.*

Chocolate Tartlets.

Four eggs, half cake of Baker's chocolate, grated; one tablespoonful corn-starch, dis-

solved in milk; three tablespoonfuls of
milk; four tablespoonfuls of white sugar;
two tablespoonfuls of vanilla; one-half teaspoonful of cinnamon and a little salt; one
heaping teaspoonful of melted butter.

Rub the chocolate smooth in the milk;
heat over the fire, and add the corn-starch
wet in more milk. Stir until thickened
and pour out. When cold beat in the
yolks and sugar with the flavoring. Bake
in open shells lining *paté*-pans. Cover
with a *méringue* made of the whites and a
little powdered sugar, when they are nearly
done, and let them color slightly. Eat
cold. — *Marion Harland.*

Chocolate Filling for Cake.

Half a cake of sweet chocolate grated,
half a cup of sweet milk, the same of
powdered sugar, the yolk of one egg, and a
tablespoonful of extract of vanilla. Stir the
chocolate in the milk, add the eggs, sugar,
and vanilla; set it in a vessel of boiling

water and stir until a stiff jelly. When cold spread it between the layers of cake. Used also as a frosting for cake. — *Sara T. Pául.*

Chocolate Wafers.

Melt two pounds of cocoa-paste in a warm iron mortar, and add to it one pound of the finest powdered sugar, and a quarter of a pound of fine vanilla sugar; pound these together with a warm pestle until the cocoa and sugar are perfectly amalgamated; if it should be too stiff add a little melted cocoa-butter or sweet oil to it and mix well in. Take a small bit of the paste in the hand and roll it into a small ball; place these as formed, out of hand, upon small sheets of glazed paper, in rows about an inch apart. When you have placed a dozen or two on a sheet take it by the ends and lift it up and down a few times, letting it touch the table each time; this motion will flatten the balls into wafers. When

cold and concreted they may be easily removed from the papers. There are various
tools for dropping these wafers to be obtained at almost any of the confectionery
supply-depots. — *Confectioner's Journal.*

Chocolate Jumbles.

Take one pound of pulverized sugar,
half a pound of butter, half a pound of
chocolate, finely grated, eight eggs, a
tablespoonful of vanilla extract, and flour
sufficient. Beat the eggs and butter to a
cream ; add and beat in the eggs, then the
grated chocolate and vanilla ; then work
in flour till you have a dough stiff enough
to roll out. Dust the table with powdered
sugar, roll the dough half an inch thick,
and cut it into pieces about four inches
long, and form them into rings by joining
the ends. Lay them at a little distance
apart on buttered baking sheets and bake
in a moderate oven. — *Confectioner's Journal.*

Chocolate Éclairs (1).

Put an ounce of butter in a saucepan on the fire, with about six tablespoonfuls of water. When beginning to boil add about two and a half ounces of flour, stirring with a wooden spoon about five minutes ; then remove from the fire and add, one by one, four eggs, stirring rapidly until each is well mixed ; then put your mixture in a cornucopia of stiff paper, with a hole in the point, through which press it on a pan, forming little shapes similar to lady-fingers. Send them to a gentle oven for about twenty minutes, or until firm ; let them become cold ; then make an incision in them the length of each through the middle. Put in a saucepan two eggs, two tablespoonfuls of corn-starch, two ounces of sugar, a glass of milk, a teaspoonful of vanilla, and stir all together on the fire. Just before beginning to boil remove from the fire and let it become cold ; then fill the inside of your *éclairs* with your cream. Melt an ounce of chocolate in a tablespoonful of water, boil half a pound of sugar as the foregoing, mix thoroughly with your chocolate, with which cover your *éclairs.* — *Pierre Caron.*

Chocolate Éclairs (2).

Prepare a batter as for Boston cream puffs, as follows: Take one pound of flour, one ounce of sugar, one quart of cold water, half a pound of butter, and sixteen eggs; put the water and butter into a bright and clean round-bottomed saucepan; place on the fire, and as soon as the water commences to boil remove it from the fire, and immediately add and rapidly stir in the flour and sugar. As soon as these are well mixed and smooth add and stir in the eggs, two or three at a time, till all are thoroughly incorporated; fill a biscuit forcer or a *méringue* bag with the batter, and press it out upon buttered baking-tins, in the same manner that you would lady-fingers, making cakes of it about five

inches long and about an inch in diameter.
Lay out these cakes at about two inches
apart on the tins, as they swell considerably in baking; bake in a hot oven. When
baked and cold make an opening on one
side of each cake and fill them with a softish custard, made as follows: Take a
quarter of a pound of powdered sugar,
two ounces of flour, the yolks of four or five
eggs, and one and a quarter pints of milk,
and a dessertspoonful of vanilla extract;
put the sugar, flour, and yolks into a
saucepan, stir them well together, then
slowly add and stir in the milk and flavor;
set it upon the fire and stir constantly till
it thickens to a smooth custard. Before
filling the cakes the tops should be dipped
and covered with chocolate icing, made as
follows: Melt one or more ounces of chocolate with half a pint of water in a saucepan, and add to it, when melted, three
ounces of fine sugar; stir and boil for three
or four minutes, then remove it from the

fire, and dip and cover the top of each cake with this chocolate icing, or they may be dipped in melted chocolate *fondant.* — *Confectioner's Journal.*

Chocolate Éclairs (3).

Prepare some batter as for cream puffs, fill a *méringue* bag with it, and press it out upon a well-buttered baking-tin in cakes about an inch wide and five inches long. Let there be two inches between each cake; bake in a quick oven fifteen to twenty minutes. When cold slit one side, open carefully and fill with the cream given above, and ice the top of each cake with chocolate prepared as follows: Melt two ounces of chocolate with a tablespoonful of water; add four ounces of powdered sugar; stir to a paste thick enough to spread without running, and coat the top of each cake with it, or dip the tops of the cakes into it; either way will do. — *Confectioner's Journal.*

CREAM, PIES, ETC.

Chocolate Cream Puffs.

Take half a pound of flour and one tea-spoonful of sugar; mix these together. Put a pint of cold water and a quarter of a pound of butter into a very clean sauce-pan, set it on the fire, and as soon as it boils remove it from the fire and throw in the flour; stir it very rapidly until well mixed and smooth; continue to beat and stir for a minute or two longer. Now let it rest for two or three minutes, and then stir and beat in with a wooden spatula eight eggs, two at a time, till all are used; the first require some little time to mix, on account of the stiffness of the paste. When all are thoroughly incorporated lay out the paste by tablespoonfuls on buttered tins, and about two inches apart each way, and bake in a quick oven for fifteen or twenty minutes. When cold cut open one side of the puff and fill it with the following cream or custard : —

Rub four ounces of sugar and four eggs to a cream ; mix two ounces of flour in gradually while stirring well. Mix and stir one ounce of grated chocolate into one quart of boiling-hot milk and a dessert-spoonful of pure extract of vanilla. Pour this into the egg mixture, set it on the fire and stir constantly till it thickens, then take it off and let it cool. — *Confectioner's Journal.*

Chocolate Blanc-Mange (1).

One quart of milk ; one-half package of gelatine, dissolved in one cup of cold water ; one cup of sugar ; three great spoonfuls grated chocolate ; vanilla to taste. Heat the milk, stir in the sugar and soaked gelatine ; strain ; add chocolate, boil ten minutes, stirring all the time. When nearly cold beat for five minutes or until it begins to stiffen. Flavor, whip up once, and put

into a wet mould. It will be firm in six
or eight hours. — *Marion Harland.*

Chocolate Blanc-mange and Cream (2).

Make the blanc-mange as directed in last
receipt. Set it to form in a mould with a
cylinder in the centre. You can improvise
one by stitching together a roll of stiff paper
just the height of the pail or bowl in which
you propose to mould your blanc-mange,
and holding it firmly in the middle of this
while you pour the mixture around it.
The paper should be well buttered. Lay
a book or other light weight on the
cylinder to keep it erect. When the blanc-
mange is turned out slip out the paper,
and fill the cavity with whipped cream,
heaping some about the base. Specks of
bright jelly enliven this dish if disposed
tastefully upon the cream. — *Marion Harland.*

Chocolate Blanc-mange (3).

Grate a teacupful of chocolate ; add to it

a pint of water and a teacup or more of sugar; let it simmer until the chocolate is all dissolved; add a quart of milk and one-third of a paper of corn-starch mixed in cold water. When the milk begins to boil stir in the corn-starch; boil it five minutes, flavor with vanilla extract, and pour into moulds. — *Sara T. Paul.*

Blanc-mange (4).

Half box gelatine; one quart milk; yolk of two eggs; one small teacupful of sugar; one large tablespoonful of vanilla; seven squares of Baker's chocolate. Dissolve the gelatine in about a gill of cold water; let it stand for two hours. Grate the chocolate fine, then dissolve it in a little of the milk, slightly warmed; scald the remainder of the milk; beat the yolks of the eggs and sugar together until very light. When the milk is well scalded, add the gelatine, chocolate, eggs, and sugar. Let this simmer gently for fifteen minutes. Strain the

mixture into a mould. Set on ice. This
blanc-mange should be thoroughly cooked.
— *Choice Receipts.*

Chocolate Custards (baked).

One quart of good milk; six eggs, yolks
and whites separated; one cup sugar; four
great spoonfuls grated chocolate; vanilla
flavoring. Scald the milk; stir in the
chocolate and simmer two minutes, to dissolve and incorporate well with the milk.
Beat up the yolks with the sugar and put
into the hot mixture. Stir for one minute
before seasoning and pouring into the cups,
which should be set ready in a pan of boiling water. They should be half sub-
merged, that the water may not bubble
over the tops. Cook slowly about twenty
minutes, or until the custards are firm.
When cold whip the whites of the eggs to
a *méringue* with a very little powdered
sugar (most *méringues* are too sweet) and
pile some upon the top of each cup. Put

a piece of red jelly on the *méringue*. — *Marion Harland*.

Chocolate Custards (boiled).

One quart of milk ; six eggs, whites and yolks separately beaten ; one cup of sugar ; four large spoonfuls grated chocolate ; vanilla to taste, a teaspoonful to the pint is a good rule. Scald the milk, stir in sugar and chocolate. Boil gently five minutes, and add the yolks. Cook five minutes more, or until it begins to thicken up well, stirring all the time. When nearly cold beat in the flavoring, and whisk all briskly for a minute before pouring into the custard-cups. Whip up the whites with a little powdered sugar, or, what is better, half a cup of currant or cranberry jelly, and heap upon the custards. — *Marion Harland*.

Chocolate Custards.

One quart of milk ; one ounce of Baker's best French chocolate ; eight eggs ; two teaspoonfuls of vanilla ; eight teaspoonfuls of white sugar. Beat the eight yolks and the two whites of the eggs until they are light. ´ Boil the milk ; when boiling stir the chocolate and the sugar into it, and then put it into a clean pitcher. Place this in a pot of boiling water ; stir one way gently all the time until it becomes a thick cream ; when cold strain it and add the vanilla ; place it in cups ; beat the whites of the eggs to a stiff froth, and add the sugar to them ; beat well, and place some of this frosting on the top of each custard. — *Choice Receipts.*

Chocolate Bavarian Cream.

Whip one pint of cream to a stiff froth, laying it on a sieve ; boil a pint of rich milk with a vanilla bean and two tablespoonfuls of sugar until it is well flavored ; then take it off the fire and add half a box of Nelson's or Coxe's gelatine, soaked for an hour in half a cupful of water in a

warm place near the range; when slightly cooled add two tablets of chocolate,
soaked and smoothed. Stir in the eggs
well beaten. When it has become quite
cold, and begins to thicken, stir it without
ceasing a few minutes, until it is very
smooth; then stir in the whipped cream
lightly until it is well mixed. Put it into
a mould or moulds, and set it on ice or in
some cool place. — *Mrs. Blair.*

Chocolate Soufflés.

Three ounces of grated chocolate, one
ounce of sugar, one ounce of butter, one
ounce of flour, one gill of milk, yolks of
three eggs, whites of four eggs. Butter
and bind around a pint and a half *soufflé-*
tin a band of paper to form a wall above
the tin, and confine the *soufflé* as it rises.
Butter also the interior of the tin.

Melt the butter in a small saucepan, stir
into it the flour, and, adding the milk, stir
all until boiling. When boiling take the

saucepan from the fire, throw into it the chocolate and the sugar, and drop in the yolks of the eggs, one by one, stirring all meantime.

Whip the whites of the eggs to a stiff froth and stir this in also very lightly.

Pour the mixture into the *soufflé*-tin, which should make it about two thirds full, and place the tin into a deep saucepan containing sufficient water to reach half-way up the sides of the form. Cover the saucepan, and drawing it aside from the fire allow the water to simmer therein for thirty minutes, keeping it all the time covered.

When steamed take the *soufflé* from the saucepan, transfer it quickly to a silver *soufflé*-dish, or fold round the tin in which it is prepared a napkin, and serve at once, carrying the dish upon a hot shovel if the dining-room be distant from the kitchen. — *Matilda Lees Dods, of the South Kensington School of Cookery.*

Chocolate Méringue.

To one quart of boiling milk add half an ounce of isinglass dissolved in hot water; add half a pound of Baker's chocolate, grated; sweeten; simmer until it becomes a rich jelly; stir while boiling. Line buttered pans with rich paste; pour in the mixture; bake until the pastry is cooked; then let it cool. Beat the whites of four eggs to a stiff froth; sweeten; spread it over the pies with a knife; bake a light brown.—*Flora Neely*.

Chocolate Creams (1).

Soak one box of gelatine in cold water enough to cover it one hour.

Put one quart of rich milk into a tin pail, and set it in a kettle with hot water to boil. Scrape two ounces of French chocolate, and mix with eight spoonfuls of sugar; wet this with two spoonfuls of the boiling milk, and rub with the bowl

of the spoon until a smooth paste, then
stir into the boiling milk ; now stir in the
gelatine, and then stir in the yolks of ten
well-beaten eggs ; stir three minutes, take
off and strain ; set in a pan of ice-water ;
stir for ten minutes, then add two spoonfuls of vanilla, and put into blanc-mange
moulds ; set away on the ice for three
hours. Serve with sugar and cream. — *M.
Parloa*.

Chocolate Creams (2).

Inside: Two cups of sugar ; one cup
of water ; one and a half tablespoonfuls
of arrow-root ; one teaspoonful of vanilla.
Outside: Half a pound of Baker's chocolate. — *Directions*. For inside : Mix the
ingredients, except the vanilla ; let them
boil from five to eight minutes ; stir all the
time. After this is taken from the fire
stir until it comes to a cream. When it
is nearly smooth add the vanilla and make
the cream into balls. For outside : Melt

the chocolate, but do not add water to it.
Roll the cream balls into the chocolate
while it is warm. — *Choice Receipts.*

Cream Chocolates.

Factitious *fondant*, or cream, is made by
mixing the finest powdered sugar with
glucose and a little extract of vanilla in a
bowl, and working them together in the
same manner as you would mix the whites
of eggs and sugar for making icing, only
there must be worked in sufficient to form
a softish paste or dough that can be rolled
into small balls with the hands ; these are
to be afterwards dipped in melted chocolate and laid on paper until the chocolate
concretes. — *Confectioner's Journal.*

Chocolate Fondant, or Cream.

Take, say, four pounds of sugar, one
quart of water, half a pound of cocoa-
paste grated, and sufficient vanilla extract
to flavor highly. Boil these to the feather,

36° by the saccharometer, 240° by thermom-
eter; then pour it upon a scrupulously
clean marble slab. When it has become
nearly cold turn or scrape in the edges,
and with a long-handled spatula work it
vigorously and steadily to and fro; it
granulates into a smooth mass; then with
a knife scrape it all together, and break
it — that is, work or knead it — with
the hands, until it forms a softish, dough-
like mass; then keep it in an earthen or
stone-ware jar or tureen, covered from the
air. It is now ready for any future operation to which you may wish to apply it. —
Confectioner's Journal.

Chocolate Charlotte Russe.

Having soaked in cold water an ounce
of gelatine, shave down three ounces of
Baker's chocolate, and mix it gradually
into a pint of cream, adding the dissolved
and strained gelatine. Set the cream,
chocolate, and gelatine over the fire, in a

porcelain kettle, and boil it slowly for three or four minutes.

Take off the fire, and let it cool. Have ready eight yolks of eggs and four whites beaten all together until very light, and stir them gradually into the mixture, in turn with half a pound of powdered sugar. Simmer the whole over the fire for a few minutes, but do not let it quite boil; then take it off, and whip it to a strong froth. Line your moulds with sponge cake, and set them on ice.

Chocolate Custard Pies.

Simmer one quart of milk; add a quarter of a pound of Baker's chocolate, grated; sweeten to taste; beat in four well-beaten eggs. Line deep pie-pans with rich paste; pour in the mixture. Bake in moderately quick oven.

Chocolate Pie (rich).

To one pint of boiling milk add one

tablespoonful of rice-flour ; the yolks of five eggs, well beaten ; a little salt ; one pint of cream ; sweeten to taste ; quarter of a pound grated chocolate (Baker's) well dried ; let them boil, stirring ; let it cool. Line deep buttered tins, pour in the mixture and bake. — *Flora Neely.*

Ice Cream (1).

Mix the yolks of four eggs with one pint of boiling milk ; one quart of cream ; four ounces of chocolate dissolved in one pint of hot water ; sweeten to taste ; flavor with extract of vanilla. Whisk thoroughly over the fire until thick and smooth ; when cool freeze.

Ice Cream (2).

To each quart of cream one tablespoonful of sweet chocolate, to be dissolved in a small quantity of cream (or water) and added when the cream is partly frozen. — *Flora Neely.*

Chocolate Ice Cream (3).

Prepare a mixture as for vanilla ice cream. Melt four ounces of chocolate in half a glass of water, on the fire; add it to your mixture, strain it through a sieve, and freeze. — *Pierre Caron.*

Chocolate Ice Cream (4).

Boil one quart of milk; grate half a pound of vanilla chocolate, and stir into the milk; let it boil until thick; add a quarter of a pound of sugar. When cool add one quart of cream; stir well and pour into the freezer. — *The Dessert Book.*

Chocolate Ice Cream (5).

To three pints of cream take one of new milk, two eggs, a teacupful of grated chocolate, two coffee-cups of powdered sugar, a teaspoonful of corn-starch and one of extract of vanilla. Beat the eggs, stir them in the milk; add the corn-starch and sugar. Let them come to a boil, take them quickly from the fire; dissolve the chocolate in a little milk over the fire, stir it all the time. When perfectly smooth mix it with the milk and eggs, then add the cream and vanilla; if not sweet enough, more sugar. When cold put it in the freezer.

Chocolate Cream Drops.

One cake of vanilla chocolate; three cups of powdered sugar; one cup of soft water; two tablespoonfuls corn-starch or arrow-root; one tablespoonful butter; two teaspoonfuls vanilla. Wash from the butter every grain of salt; stir the sugar and water together; mix in the corn-starch and bring to a boil, stirring constantly to induce granulation. Boil about ten minutes, when add the butter. Take from the fire and beat as you would eggs until it begins to look like granulated cream. Put in the vanilla; butter your hands well, make the cream into balls about the size of a large marble, and lay upon a greased dish.

Meanwhile the chocolate should have been melted by putting it (grated fine) into a tin pail or saucepan and plunging it into another of boiling water. When it is a black syrup add about two tablespoonfuls of sugar to it, beat smooth, turn out upon a *hot* dish, and roll the cream balls in it until sufficiently coated. Lay upon a cold dish to dry, taking care that they do not touch one another. — *Marion Harland.*

Chocolate Caramels (1).

One cup rich, sweet cream ; one cup brown sugar ; one cup white sugar ; seven tablespoonfuls vanilla chocolate ; one tablespoonful corn-starch stirred into the cream ; one tablespoonful butter ; vanilla flavoring ; soda the size of a pea stirred into cream. Boil all the ingredients except the chocolate and vanilla extract half an hour, stirring to prevent burning. Reserve half of the cream and wet up the chocolate in it, adding a very little water if necessary. Draw the saucepan to the side of the range, and stir this in well; put back on the fire, and boil ten minutes longer, quite fast, stirring constantly. When it makes a hard, glossy coat on the spoon it is done. Add the vanilla after taking it from the range. Turn into shallow dishes well buttered. When cold enough to retain the impression of the knife cut into squares. — *Marion Harland.*

Chocolate Caramels (2).

One cupful of best syrup; one cupful of brown sugar; one cupful of white sugar; two cupfuls of grated chocolate; two cupfuls of cream vanilla; one teaspoonful of flour mixed with cream. Rub the chocolate to a smooth paste with a little of the cream; boil all together half an hour, and pour it into flat dishes to cool. Mark it with a knife into little squares when it is cool enough. — *Mrs. Mary F. Henderson.*

Cream Chocolate Caramel (3.)

Make a six-pound batch of chocolate car-

amel; pour it out in as square a form as
possible upon a greased marble slab (without iron bars); let it spread out as thin as
it will, and when it becomes cold run the
candy sword under it in order to loosen it
from the slab; then mark it crosswise
through the centre of the batch, and pour
thickly melted *fondant* over one-half the
surface; then take the uncovered half by
the end, using both hands, and quickly
throw it over the creamed portion. Press
this top sheet down upon the other all
around the edges, then, with a caramel
cutter, cut the batch into small square
tablets. In this manner the cream is enclosed in the centre of each tablet. — *Confectioner's Journal.*

Chocolate Candy.

One cup of molasses, two of sugar, one
of milk, one-half of chocolate, a piece of
butter half the size of an egg.

Boil the milk and molasses together,

scrape the chocolate fine, and mix with just enough of the boiling milk and molasses to moisten ; rub it perfectly smooth, then, with the sugar, stir into the boiling liquid ; add the butter, and boil twenty minutes. Try as molasses candy, and if it hardens pour into a buttered dish. Cut the same as nut-candy. — *M. Parloa.*

Crême de Cacao.

Infuse five ounces of Caracas cocoanibs, crushed ; one bean of Vera Cruz vanilla, split and cut into small pieces ; quarter ounce of cinnamon, and one drop of essence of almond, in one quart of brandy, or deodorized alcohol, for ten days. Strain, press ; then filter clear, and add one quart of clarified syrup. Bottle and cork well. — *Confectioner's Journal.*

Chocolate Parfait Amour.

Dissolve half a pound of chocolate highly flavored with vanilla in sufficient water. In a bottle of brandy digest one ounce of bruised cinnamon, half an ounce of cloves, and a pinch of salt. In three days add the dissolved chocolate; macerate one week, closely corked; then strain clear. — *Confectioner's Journal.*

Bavaroise au Chocolate.

Mix one egg and two ounces of powdered sugar with one pint of milk or cream; place it on the fire and stir until it is about to boil; then instantly remove and add a gill of well-made, rich chocolate and a teaspoonful of extract of vanilla. Pour it into pint tumblers and serve. Zwieback, nice and fresh, is generally served with the chocolate *bavaroise.* — *Confectioner's Journal.*

Chocolate Syrup.

Mix eight ounces of chocolate in one quart of water, and stir, and melt thoroughly over a slow fire. Strain and add four pounds of white sugar. — *Confectioner's Journal.*

Chocolate Syrup for Soda Water.

Baker's chocolate (plain), four ounces; boiling water, four ounces; water, twenty-eight ounces; sugar, thirty ounces; extract of vanilla, one-half ounce. Cut the chocolate into small pieces, then add the boiling water, and stir briskly until the mixture forms into a thick paste, and assumes a smooth and uniform appearance; then slowly add the remainder of the water, stirring at the same time, and set aside until cold. After cooling thoroughly, a layer of solid grease forms over the surface, which is to be carefully removed by skimming. After this is completed add the sugar, dissolved by the aid of a gentle heat, and allow the whole to come to a boil. Then strain and add the extract of vanilla. This forms a syrup which is perfect. It possesses the pure, rich flavor of the chocolate without the unpleasant taste which is obtained if the solid fat is not removed. — *M. Michaelis.*

Chocolate Icing or Coating.

Put one pound of the best sugar in a
copper pan and boil to the blow, or thirty-
four degrees ; place the bottom of the pan in
cold water (contained in a saucepan) to cool,
until the sugar begins to set at the bottom
and sides of the pan. Put a quarter of a
pound of fine chocolate or cocoa paste with
half a gill of water in a pan ; place it in the
mouth of the oven, or on a very slow fire,
until it is thoroughly melted, stirring constantly ; add half a gill of simple syrup, and
work until it is entirely smooth, then add it
to the boiled sugar. Mix well and ice or
cover your cakes. In a few minutes they
will become dry.— *Confectioner's Journal.*

Chocolate Whip (1).

One ounce of cocoa-paste, scraped fine,
added to one quart of rich cream and half
a pound of pulverized sugar ; place on the
pan and bring it to the boiling-point, stir-

ring constantly with a whisk ; then remove it, and when cold add the whites of four eggs and whisk briskly; remove the froth with a perforated skimmer, and lay it upon a hair sieve to drain. When you have sufficient froth, or whip, fill your glasses or cups three-fourths full of the cream and pile the whip on the top of them ; sprinkle a little vanilla sugar, or powdered cinnamon, on the whip, and serve.

Chocolate Whip (2).

Dissolve two ounces of cocoa-paste, on a moderate fire, in half a tumbler of boiling water, and when cold add it to the cream together with six ounces of fine sugar. Whip and finish as above.

Chocolate Drops, with Nonpareils.

Warm some sweet chocolate by pounding it in a hot iron mortar ; when it is reduced to a malleable paste make it into balls, about the size of a small marble, by rolling a little in the hand. Place them

on sheets of white paper about an inch
apart.   When the sheet is covered, take it
by the corners and lift it up and down,
letting it touch the table each time, which
will flatten them.   Cover the surface entirely with white nonpareils, and shake off
the surplus one.   The bottom of the drops
should be about as broad as a five-cent piece.
— *Confectioner's Journal.*

ADVERTISEMENT.

Established in the Year 1780.

***

WALTER BAKER & CO.,

DORCHESTER, MASS.,

MANUFACTURERS OF

CHOCOLATE, BROMA, AND OTHER PREPARATIONS FROM COCOA.

***

SEVENTEEN MEDALS AND DIPLOMAS RECEIVED FROM THE GREAT IN-TERNATIONAL AND OTHER EXHIBITIONS.

Frequent analyses have been made, under the direction of Boards of Health and sanitary associations in our large cities, to determine the purity of chocolate and cocoa preparations sold in this country, and in every such analysis the articles manufactured by

WALTER BAKER & CO.,

are reported to be entirely pure and free from the admixture of deleterious substances.

BAKER'S PREMIUM No. 1 CHOCOLATE,

In 1-lb. packages, blue wrapper, yellow label,

Is the fresh roasted cocoa-beans carefully selected and prepared, then moulded into cakes. It is the very best preparation of plain chocolate in the market for family use. Celebrated for more than a century as a nutritive, salutary, and delicious beverage.

BAKER'S VANILLA CHOCOLATE,

In 1-2 lb. packages,

Is guaranteed to consist solely of choice cocoa and sugar, flavored with pure vanilla beans. Particular care is taken in its preparation, and a trial will convince one that it is really a delicious article for eating or drinking. It is equal to any of the imported chocolates. For tourists and those who wish a very pleasant article for eating dry, and without any preparation, it is the best.

GERMAN SWEET CHOCOLATE,

In 1-4 lb. packages,

Is one of the most popular sweet chocolates sold anywhere. It is palatable, nutritious, and healthful. It is a great favorite with children, and an excellent substitute for much of the confectionery now offered to the public.

Beware of Imitations. The Genuine is Stamped S. German, Dorchester, Mass.

158   ADVERTISEMENT.

BAKER'S PREPARED COCOA,

In 1-2 pound packages, yellow label,

Is a perfectly pure and refreshing beverage, prepared exclusively from selected cocoa. It is safely recommended to those who wish a wholesome preparation, combining all the properties of the cocoa-beans. It has for nearly a century been a standard article of consumption.

BAKER'S CRACKED COCOA, OR COCOA NIBS,

In 1-2 and 1 lb. packages and 6 and 10 lb. bags,

Is the fresh roasted bean cracked into small pieces. It contains no admixture, and presents the full flavor of the cocoa-bean in all its natural fragrance and purity. When properly prepared it is one of the most economical drinks. Dr. Lankester says cocoa contains as much flesh-forming matter as beef.

BAKER'S BROMA,

In 1-2 lb. packages (tin),

Is a preparation of pure cocoa and other highly nutritious substances, pleasantly flavored and sweetened. It contains a large proportion of theobromine, and possesses powerful restorative qualities. Its delicacy of flavor and perfect solubility have made it a favorite drink among thousands.

The *Medical Gazette* says: " Broma, an admirable preparation, alike agreeable to the well and the sick, has acquired a reputation which we think it certainly deserves. Hospitals, infirmaries, and households generally, should always be provided with it. When gruel, arrow-root, and many other things ordinarily resorted to for patients are of no utility, broma is sometimes relished and assimilates well. Medical men of all shades of opinion recommend it to their patients instead of tea or coffee.

160 ADVERTISEMENT.

BAKER'S BREAKFAST COCOA,

In 1-2 lb. packages (tin),

Is made from selected cocoa, with the excess of butter of cacao removed, and guaranteed to be absolutely pure. It is more than three times the strength of other cocoas, making an economical, excellent, and delicious beverage for breakfast or supper,

Costing less than One Cent a Cup.

A general favorite with all who have tried it. When purchasing be sure that your grocer supplies you with *BAKER'S BREAKFAST COCOA*, as there are imitations offered at a lower price.

A prominent and experienced New York physician says: "Experience from many years' practice in the treatment of lung diseases has convinced me that, as an article of diet for those suffering *with any form of consumption*, chocolate is far preferable to tea or coffee; in fact, the two last-mentioned articles are injurious in many cases, while chocolate, being an aliment and analeptic, is particularly serviceable where digestion has been impaired by disease. Having examined several specimens of chocolate I find that *Baker's* may be conscientiously recommended to invalids."

COCOA-BUTTER,

In 1-4 lb. cakes.

One-half the weight of the cocoa-beans consists of a fat called Cocoa-Butter, from its resemblance to ordinary butter. It is considered a great value as a nutritious, strengthening ·tonic, being preferred to cod-liver oil and other nauseous fats so often used in pulmonary complaints. As a soothing application to chapped hands and lips and all irritated surfaces Cocoa-Butter has no equal, making the skin remarkably soft and smooth. Many who have used it say they would not be without it, it is such a useful article to have in every household.

COCOA-SHELLS,

In 1-lb. packages.

Cocoa-Shells are the thin outer covering of the beans. They have a flavor similar to but milder than cocoa. Their very low price places them within the reach of all, and as a pleasant and healthy drink they are considered superior to tea and coffee.

Packed *only* in one-pound papers, with our label and name on them.

RACAHOUT DES ARABES,

In boxes, 6 lbs. each, — 1-2 lb. bottles.

This celebrated preparation is a most nutritious substance, and has become indispensable as an article of diet for children, convalescents, ladies, and delicate or aged persons; is composed of the best nutritive and restoring substances, suitable for the most delicate system. It is now a *favorite breakfast beverage for ladies and young persons*, to whom it gives freshness and *embonpoint*. It has solved the problem of medicine, by imparting something which is easily digestible, and at the same time *free from the exciting qualities* of coffee and tea, — thus making it especially desirable for nervous persons, or those afflicted with weak stomachs.

Racahout has a very agreeable flavor, is easily prepared, and has received the *commendation of eminent Physicians*, as being the best article known for convalescents, and all persons desiring a *light, digestible, nourishing, and strengthening food.*

GOODS FOR CONFECTIONERS' USE.

W. BAKER & CO.'S CARACAS LIQUOR, in cases, 100 lbs. each.

W. BAKER & CO.'S MARACAIBO LIQUOR, in cases, 100 lbs. each.

EAGLE PURE CHOCOLATE LIQUOR, in cases, 100 lbs. each.

ALSO

W. BAKER & CO.'S COCOA and SHELLS, in bags, 12 and 25 lbs. each.

W. BAKER & CO.'S COCOA-PASTE, in boxes, 12 lbs. each.

VANILLA CHOCOLATE TABLETS (for eating), in boxes, 7 lbs. each.

ADVERTISEMENT. 165

MEDALS AND DIPLOMAS

AWARDED TO

WALTER BAKER & CO.

The World's Industrial Exposition, New Orleans, 1884.
Southern Exposition, Louisville, 1883.
Mechanics' Institute, Boston, 1878.
Paris Exposition, 1878.
Mechanics' Institute, San Francisco, 1877.
U.S. Centennial Exhibition, 1876.
Vienna Exposition, 1873.
Mechanics' Institute, New Orleans, 1871.
Paris Exposition, 1867.
Mechanics' Institute, Cincinnati, 1855.
Maryland Institute, 1853.
Crystal Palace Exhibition, N.Y., 1853.
American Institute, N.Y., 1853.
Franklin Institute, Philadelphia, 1853.
Mechanics' Institute, Boston, 1853.
Maryland Institute, Baltimore, 1852.
Smithsonian Institution, Washington.